Anxiety Workbook

Stop Worrying And Regain Control Of Your Life. Learn How To Manage And Overcome Panic Attacks, Phobias, Social Anxiety And Depression

Howard PhD, Amanda

Text Copyright © 2019 [Howard PhD, Amanda]

All rights reserved. No part of this guide may be reproduced in any form without permission in writing from the publisher except in the case of brief quotations embodied in critical articles or reviews.

Legal & Disclaimer

The information contained in this book and its contents is not designed to replace or take the place of any form of medical or professional advice; and is not meant to replace the need for independent medical, financial, legal or other professional advice or services, as may be required. The content and information in this book has been provided for educational and entertainment purposes only. The content and information contained in this book has been compiled from sources deemed reliable, and it is accurate to the best of the Author's knowledge, information and belief. However, the Author cannot guarantee its accuracy and validity and cannot be held liable for any errors and/or omissions. Further, changes are periodically made to this book as and when needed. Where appropriate and/or necessary, you must consult a professional (including but not limited to your doctor, attorney, financial advisor or such other professional advisor) before using any of the suggested remedies, techniques, or information in this book.

Upon using the contents and information contained in this book, you agree to hold harmless the Author from and against any damages, costs, and expenses, including any legal fees potentially resulting from the application of any of the information provided by this book. This disclaimer applies to any loss, damages or injury caused by the use and application, whether directly or indirectly, of any advice or information presented, whether for breach of contract, tort, negligence, personal injury, criminal intent, or under any other cause of action.

You agree to accept all risks of using the information presented inside this book. You agree that by continuing to read this book, where appropriate and/or necessary, you shall consult a professional (including but not limited to your doctor, attorney, or financial advisor or such other advisor as needed) before using any of the suggested remedies, techniques, or information in this book.

TABLE OF CONTENTS

Introduction 1
Chapter 1: Major Causes of Anxiety Disorder 5
Chapter 2: Practicing Mindfulness to Overcome Anxiety 15
Chapter 3: How to Manage Thoughts to Control Anxiety 22
Chapter 4: How to Manage Activities to Reduce Anxiety................. 30
Chapter 5: Ways to Find Instant Calm and Overcome Anxiety........ 37
Chapter 6: Medications and Herbs to Treat Anxiety 44
Chapter 7: Aromatherapy and Acupuncture 53
Chapter 8: Behavioral Therapy for Anxiety Disorders 64
Chapter 9: Lifestyle Changes to take back Control 71
Chapter 10: Panic Attacks 79
Chapter 11: Phobias 89
Chapter 12: Social Anxiety 98
Chapter 13: Depression Link 105
Conclusion 112
References 114

INTRODUCTION

The average modern person lives most of his or her life under pressure; we are either chasing after something or something is chasing after us. And we live under the assumption that we must find a solution now or everything is lost! Many of us use our bedtime not just for sleep but for ruminating over worst-case scenarios. We fall asleep daily with our minds filled with a lot of negative thoughts and what-ifs. And when we wake up, we go right back to our last thoughts of fear, worry, and concerns about our health and fitness, unpaid bills, relationship dramas, deadlines, work schedules, and so on. Our inability to properly manage such pressures can start to take its toll on our day-to-day functions. Eventually, this can lead to constant stress and anxiety disorders.

A significant number of anxiety disorders can also be traced to holding on tightly to past traumas. When a person continually relives a past event and projects the same past feelings to present and future events, it becomes difficult for such a person to live and function optimally. This is not a pleasant mental and physical position to be. Its impacts are debilitating and can render an otherwise productive person almost helpless and, in some cases, useless. But beyond these, it can also lead to depression – a situation where the individual becomes a threat to themselves, to others, or both.

Thankfully, there are ways to help people manage both daily pressure-induced anxieties and past trauma-induced anxieties. And these ways are not only limited to clinical treatments but also behavior modification and lifestyle changes. This book will expose you to several helpful ways that have been proven to provide both short-term and long-term relief from anxiety even without medications. You can find instant calm in situations that trigger anxious thoughts and feelings in you if you apply some of the simple techniques described in this book.

Anxiety is our mind and body's response to a threat. When we get anxious whether from real or perceived threats, different parts of our bodies receive signals from our brain to prepare us to handle the situation either by going offensive (fight) or by taking defense (flight). This is a natural defense mechanism that is activated each time we perceive a threat. The problem is that a lot of the times these threats are unreal but since our brains can't differentiate between real and perceived threats, it revs up our body system anyway if we'll need to protect ourselves from whatever that seems to be threatening our survival. It is like having your foot stuck on your car's accelerator with the brakes on; the car is not moving an inch yet the engine is on overdrive! Over time, our natural defense mechanism weakens and opens us up to mental health disorders such as anxiety and depression.

Training the brain to relax and to not continuously activate our fight or flight response is the key to overcoming unnecessary fears, anxiety, and other mental health disorders. It is not an easy task to accomplish especially when you live in a world that seems to be in a constant hurry. Getting yourself to slow down, to become mindful of what you are thinking and doing at the moment, and be in tune with what is happening in your body will take some practice. However, mastering these things is one of the lasting solutions to overcoming anxiety and that is the central idea of this book.

The solution to overcoming anxiety does not lie in reading books about anxiety. The problem with managing and coping with anxiety is not a shortage or lack of knowledge about what to do. Many of us already have a fairly good idea of what to do. And for those who don't, you'll find sufficient advice and useful information in this book. But applying what you read is where the rubber meets the road. And being consistent about its application is what produces the result you seek. Although this book will show you ways to find instant calm when you are in a heightened state of anxiety, there is still a need to remain consistent in putting into practice the other techniques that can help you find lasting solutions to anxiety disorders. I believe that the tendency to seek quick fixes is an indication of anxiousness and that can lead to discarding useful information because they don't seem to proffer immediate solutions. Your goal shouldn't be just to finish reading this book; instead, it should be to be fully equipped with the right knowledge to properly manage stress-inducing activities and dealing with anxiety disorders.

I'll share with you scientifically proven techniques that can help you slow down and avoid all the unnecessary rush that is usually associated with living in our modern world and which can easily push you down the path of anxious thoughts and actions. While medications or drugs can be used to manage and treat anxiety, not many of us can endure the unpleasant side effects associated with these medications. Besides, the techniques for coping with anxiety which I share in this book have little to no side effects at all.

That said, I must point out that there is no quick fix that can magically dispel all problems of anxiety in one fell swoop. Save for a miracle – which this book doesn't promise – you'll need time and continuous implementation of the different techniques and strategies outlined in the pages of this book to overcome anxiety disorder. You'll also discover how to tweak and redesign some of your daily activities to help you reduce stress. As you study and apply the techniques shared in this book, you will begin to notice a gradual shift in how you respond emotionally to psycho-social events that can trigger anxious thoughts. Your reactions to events, situations, and people will become more deliberate and more intelligent. Before long, you would have regained complete control of your life and enjoy the freedom that comes from being in charge of your physical and mental health.

CHAPTER 1: MAJOR CAUSES OF ANXIETY DISORDER

In the time of our forefathers, they were constantly facing attacks from wild animals and enemies. As a result, they needed a form of internal disturbance to stay alert and alive. During their time, anxiety was normal as it revealed a potential threat to their existence. It allowed them to escape wild animals and other threats to their lives.

We are no more living in caves and chasing animals all around. However, man is yet to evolve as simple things that might not be life-threatening triggers anxiety. If you think of it, anxiety is normal as it prepares you for danger and keeps you alert in the face of life-threatening situations.

Anxiety can be seen as the normal reaction of the body to danger. It is triggered under pressure or when facing a daunting situation. It is normal to be anxious when going for an interview, sitting for an exam or even meeting someone for the first time. Mild anxiety is a normal part of life which is no cause for alarm. It can mean the difference between life and death as it keeps you on your toes, activate the fight or flight response like it did during the time of our ancestors. It can motivate you to do your best and solve life issues.

However, when anxiety gets in the way of your day to day activity such that it cripples you, affects your daily function, it is no longer normal anxiety but a disorder – anxiety disorder.

Anxiety disorder is a group of related medical disorders with varying symptoms. It is one of the most common mental health disorders. It comes in various forms and could vary from one person to the other. One person might have a problem talking to strangers while another person might not be comfortable mingling at parties. Someone else might have a fear of flying with disturbing and uncontrollable thoughts. Another person might be baffled with the fear of everything and anything. All in all, anxiety disorder is characterized by an irrational fear or worry that is baseless, concerning a situation at present or in the future.

Bear in mind that anxiety disorder can be crippling. It holds people back from living life to the fullest and fulfilling their potentials. It robs people of achieving their goals, making them live under the irrational fears of things that do not exist. The bright side is that it is a pretty common form of mental disorder hence, you are not alone. Another good news is that there are many treatment methods for anxiety disorder. This is scheduled for a later chapter in this book.

How to Know if you have Anxiety Disorder

Check out the following signs that reveal the presence of anxiety disorder. If any of the following signs will not go away, you might be experiencing an anxiety disorder.

- A constant feeling of worry, stress and being on edge.
- Inability to go about your day to day responsibility like family, school, and work
- Being plagued and crippled by baseless fears that will not go away.
- Staying away from situations because they make you nervous.
- Feeling or expecting something bad to happen
- The irrational beating of the heart (palpitation) due to no specific cause

In addition to the above, other major symptoms of anxiety disorders are:

- Expecting the worst
- Difficulty concentrating
- A tensed feeling
- Feeling irritable
- Sweating
- trembling
- Headache
- Migraine
- Frequent urination
- Insomnia
- Dizziness

Forms of Anxiety Disorder

Anxiety disorder comes in many forms. We will shed light on the major forms below:

Generalized anxiety disorder (GAD)

This is the most common form of anxiety disorder; It involves general worry, concern, and fear about everyday activities. It also involves an irrational fear that evil is on the way. Victims are characterized by intense worry and anxiety which are many time baseless. Victims of generalized anxiety disorder often experience physical symptoms like restlessness, migraine, and insomnia.

Obsessive-Compulsive Disorder

If you have thoughts that are unhelpful, yet impossible to stop, you are suffering from obsessive-compulsive disorder (OCD). It is an irrational, recurring obsession, for instance, the compulsion to have your sitting room arranged in a particular order. It might be worrying that you forgot to switch off the washing machine etc. It might also be fear of germs which makes you wash your hands and clothes every time.

Phobia or Irrational Fears

Phobia is a baseless and excessive fear of a particular object, thing, activity, place or person. This fear is often baseless because the object or place of fear, most of the time is harmless. Phobia is characterized by:

- Uncontrolled anxiety and feeling of helplessness when faced with the object of dread
- Severe paralysis on exposure to the dreaded object or thing
- A compulsive avoidance of the object of dread.

Phobias range from fear of the place to people, to animals, clowns, and even germs. Some people are afraid of snakes and spiders. It could be fear of enclosed places or meeting new people. We will explore more about phobias in the coming chapter. Victims of phobia go to extreme length to avoid what they fear which only ends up strengthening the phobia.

Social Anxiety Disorder

Fear and anxiety of appearing in public, meeting new people, etc., is called social anxiety, it is an intense worry that you will make a mess of yourself in public and be humiliated. It manifests itself as an extreme form of shyness which makes the victim avoid all forms of social appearance. As a result, victims avoid going to parties, meeting new people, asking questions in public gatherings, etc.

Separation Anxiety Disorder

It could be normal to be anxious for a while when separated from loved ones. However, if the separation lingers such that its graduates and paralyzes the victim, it is known as a separation anxiety disorder. A child that cries hours after the mum drops her off at the school might be suffering from a separation anxiety disorder.

Post-Traumatic Stress Disorder

Also known as PTSD, it is a severe form of anxiety disorder caused by a life-threatening situation. Victims of terrorist attacks, domestic violence, victims of narcissist partners, rape victims, etc. could experience PTSD. It springs up and paralyzes the victim when they remember the traumatic experience. Symptoms could include isolation, avoidance situation, nightmares, nervousness, being easily startled, etc.

Causes of Anxiety Disorders

Ranging from genetic factors to environmental factors, there are many causes of anxiety disorder. We will shed light on what you have to know about the causes in this chapter.

Genetics

One of the major determining factors that influence the onset of anxiety is your gene. Just like many other health conditions like cancer, high blood pressure, etc. your lineage (ancestors) can determine if you will develop anxiety or not.

In other words, as long as some genetic markers are passed down from the parents, there is a high probability of developing an anxiety disorder. This, when combined with many environmental factors could influence the onset of anxiety disorder.

According to studies, women are prone to developing anxiety, even though this condition develops around age 30.

The Brain Structure

There is a collection of certain parts of the brain structure known as the limbic system. It controls and helps regulate many emotional needs.

The Amygdala

This is the part of our limbic system in control of fear or flight. It also helps in the formation and integration of memory and emotions. Knowing the operation of the amygdala is central to understanding and discerning fear. This reveals why many victims of anxiety disorder show excessive amygdale activities when faced with negative emotions. These activities are the ones responsible for negative interpretations of things and situations that cause anxiety disorder.

This is why people with anxiety disorder interpret normal activity as life-threatening which manifests in their behaviors.

Gray Matter

In addition to the amygdala, the volume of grey matter is another factor linked to anxiety disorder. Many victims of anxiety showed an increased volume of grey matters in some parts of their brains. The right putamen, for instance, showed increased volume.

According to research, people that were exposed to childhood trauma or maltreatment showed increased volume in their right putamen. This reveals a cogent fact that a child that experienced maltreatment will likely have an enlarged volume of the gray matter which will manifest in the form of social anxiety disorder.

Other causes of Anxiety Disorder

There is no singular cause of anxiety disorder. In addition to the brain factor discussed above, other causes of anxiety disorder are family background, life experiences, and social influence.

Life Experiences

While genetic and biological factors are one of the major factors that contribute to the onset of anxiety disorder, environmental, social and complex psychological factors also influence it. A good example is a trauma.

Trauma and Anxiety Disorder

As discussed above, a child that was abused or exposed to a traumatic event has a high tendency of developing an anxiety disorder. A traumatic experience like narcissistic abuse, rape, neglect, mental and physical abuse, divorce, isolation all contribute.

It is normal to feel anxious after going through some hard life experiences that make us feel uncertain, humiliated or unwillingly to trust others. Life events that cause loss of loved ones, entrapment, dangers, humiliations, etc., contribute to the anxiety.

This is why victims of anxiety disorder do not interpret events accurately.

Rather, they associated threats and dangers to seemingly harmless life experiences.

This is why in treating anxiety disorder, getting to the root of the matter via probing social and family history is important. Addressing this is key to treating anxiety disorder.

Lifestyle Choices

In addition to gene and childhood traumatic experiences, other factors that could be responsible for anxiety disorder are:

Caffeine:

Excessive reliance on caffeine and other addictive substance can trigger a feeling of anxiety, worry, and nervousness. We put pressure on ourselves to meet a deadline, meet expectations and obligations. This makes us push ourselves to surmount the fear of being inadequate.

Excessive reliance on sources of caffeine like soda, energy drinks, tea, etc., can trigger a feeling of helplessness and anxiety in others.

Relationships

A romantic relationship should be a source of joy. There are times when issues in a relationship, however, triggers pain which results in anxiety. A relationship with a narcissist, for instance, is bound to make the partner miserable. This is due to the constant humiliation and abuse by the partner. This, without a doubt, could trigger a feeling of anxiety in partners.

Job Stress

Many people face a lot of stress in their work which could lead to anxiety disorder. Excessive high expectation places great demands on people which could threaten job security thereby triggering anxiety. The quest to meet demands and expectations also leads to worry and anxiety.

Seeking for a job as well could also trigger a feeling of anxiety. When faced with candidates who are more qualified, it leads to the anxiety of not being up to the task, triggering anxiety disorder.

Health Issues

A disturbing health diagnosis like a tumor, cancer, or chronic illness could trigger anxiety or feeling of uneasiness. This is understandable because receiving such shocking news causes a negative feeling and a great level of discomfort.

The thought of having a degenerative health issue that could shorten one's lifespan is enough to trigger anxiety.

Social Events

Many people are greatly uncomfortable in the presence of strangers. They dread anything that will put them in the spotlight due to an irrational fear of making a fool of themselves. As a result of this, they could be uneasy or restless in social gatherings like parties or get together.

This class of people will rather withdraw to the last seat at the restaurant or hide in a corner to prevent interaction with strangers.

Stress

Stress is one of the leading causes of anxiety. The root of all causes of anxiety goes back to stress which in turn triggers anxiety. Anyone could be anxious at the thought of missing a flight or flopping at a thesis presentation. Long term stress, however, triggers anxiety which brings about other unwanted health problems.

Some people resort to a harmful coping mechanism for stress like alcohol, which worsens matters. Stress also causes a lack of sleep and difficulty concentration which worsens anxiety.

All in all, when we are exposed to severe stress, there is a high tendency to develop an anxiety disorder.

In summary

There are many causes of anxiety. If you can identify the cause, half of it is solved. This can lead you in the right direction in getting help. For instance, a person in a relationship with a narcissist only needs to look for ways to handle a narcissistic partner. In doing this, she can overcome the anxiety and stress that comes from being in such an abusive relationship.

CHAPTER 2: PRACTICING MINDFULNESS TO OVERCOME ANXIETY

In this chapter, you will be learning how to break yourself loose from the shackles of obsessive worrying and anxiety by taking some time to practice the simple exercise referred to here as "mindfulness".

You see, the ability to think is one of the distinguishing factors that are unique to humans and makes us distinct from animals. This thinking faculty in us is what gives us the power to sustain an idea and make real products and render useful services from it. This same ability, however, exposes us to a different type of fear that is not known anywhere in the animal kingdom but only in human society. This type of fear is known as psychological fear.

Psychological fear comes from the knowledge of something that has happened in the past and has the possibility of recurring again in the future. The ability to think recreates a vivid picture of how it happened the last time in our imagination, whether it had happened to us personally in the past or we read about how it happened somewhere or to someone. Animals do not have this gift of creative imagination and that is why they do not experience the fear attached.

A problem with thinking occurs when you confuse thoughts about things with things themselves. It's easier to think of an imaginary frog and knows that the frog in your head is not the same as a real frog. But when your mind gives you something physically non-existent, such as your self-esteem, it is difficult to notice the difference.

Everyone has negative thoughts sometimes and may even at a point or another believe them. However, not everyone develops persistent anxiety, depression, or emotional distress. An important question arises: what controls and determines whether these thoughts will go away, or whether prolonged and intense distress will develop?

You see, thoughts of self-esteem are no more real than an imaginary frog. If you switch to the "be" mode, you will see it much more clearly. You can distance yourself and observe the thoughts and feelings that come to your mind and leave it like sounds, tastes, and types. Therefore, when your thought gives out: "I feel like a failure", you should not perceive this as reality and fall into inevitable rumination.

This is not trying to say that animals do not fear, but rather they only experience the fear that has to do with a current event or occurrence. Birds migrate in large numbers when they notice a bad weather approaching, that is fear but unlike psychological fear, it is not based on imagination but at the warning of their instinct.

There is another interesting fact about psychological fear. It is the fact that though the event you are thinking about is just a figment of your imagination and not a real occurrence at the moment, the human body responds just as it would have if the event was happening.

Anxiety often results in an uncoordinated state of the human mind and the body, where the thoughts patterns move in one direction, the emotions move on the other, and physical sensations also go in another direction. The life of the person seems fragmented. Simply put, even though the event might not be happening in the present, the effect is real on the person and ends up scattering or distorting his/her current perception of reality.

When a person is anxious, the mind moves freely and separates from the body and the body ends up suffering the effect of this erratic flow of the human mind. The thoughts, emotions and physical sensations vibrate at different "frequencies". The good news, however, is that mindfulness as a tool can help bring balance.

Wikipedia defines mindfulness as "the psychological process of purposely bringing one's attention to experiences occurring in the present moment." Paying attention to what is happening during the process of thinking and realizing when and how your mind wanders, intending to bring it back to the present reality is what *Mindfulness* entails. It is very powerful in keeping the elements of thoughts, emotions and physical actions in perfect harmony.

A lot of people get lost in thoughts and the process of thinking has almost become an unconscious one for them. Mindfulness is a skill that can be learned and developed over time if it is intentionally cultivated by frequent practice. It may seem difficult to engage in at first, this is because an average mind tends to disperse quickly and get lost in thoughts about the future, and every possible thing that can go wrong. However, it is a worthwhile engagement considering the effect of our thought on our daily life and by extension, our future.

What does mindfulness have to do with anxiety?

Anxiety occurs when you are focusing attention on all the uncertainties while neglecting other possibilities. It is not uncommon to find people caught up in what-if scenarios, working with hypotheses and situations beyond their control when it would have been easier to have a better and a more positive outlook rather than the energy-sapping negative thoughts.

Imagine a businessman that has an important presentation before his would-be investors the next day suddenly falling into the unnecessary panic attack. He will most probably begin to think about everything that could go wrong before, during and after the presentation. He would never think about so many other good things that could go right. Thoughts such as forgetting the flash drive, not able to speak properly, the slides not opening on the computer, the problem with the public address system or eventually making a very poor presentation that will not impress the investors, etc.

It would have been a more productive and worthwhile engagement if that same mental energy is channeled into preparing for his presentation. He could focus on the present moment and the possibility of maximizing every moment he will spend in front of his viewers and ultimately make a good presentation that will boost the investors' confidence in his ability to manage their resources. This type of ugly scenario can be properly managed by learning and applying mindfulness.

Mindfulness gives you full control and the mind ends up being a useful tool rather than a troublesome master. It can be willingly engaged, for example, one of the easiest ways to start engaging in mindful thinking is during a meal. During the process of eating, pay closer attention to the food on your plate, taking into cognizance its colors, textures, flavors, and how it feels when you chew. This is far better than simply gorging in the food without any particular interest in the whole process. This is how to engage your mind positively.

One great thing about mindfulness is to be aware that you are thinking. Your thought is something you produce willingly and not something that should go on spontaneously or accidentally like a train running without a brake.

When you are engaged in mindful thinking, you will be in charge of your thoughts and reprogramming your thought patterns. Past thought patterns that had been built through a previous lifestyle, experiences, culture, and core-relationships such as with parents, school, family and every person who had played an important role in your life and upbringing. Many of these thought patterns are toxic to your mental health and so must be eliminated by all means.

Dealing with Experiential avoidance through Mindfulness

People who are suffering from anxiety often exhibit certain behavioral patterns that are referred to as "experiential avoidance". This occurs when such a person is haunted by the memories of an event that happened in the past and does not want to be in touch with certain elements that characterized that experience. Some such elements could be body sensations, emotions, thoughts, sight, etc.

Unfortunately, when you put effort into avoiding such thoughts like this, it ends up producing the opposite of what you want and such a person becomes increasingly anxious and out of control. People exhibiting standard experiential avoidance behavior are much more likely to develop phobias.

They will try to escape in the face of an unexpected panic attack, far more than those who can control their minds. Suppression of thoughts and feelings contribute to the development and maintenance of generalized anxiety disorder, specific phobias, and posttraumatic stress disorder.

How to apply mindfulness in dealing with Anxiety?

The process of recovering from anxiety through mindfulness is known as "integration" where all the separate, isolated or denied parts must be reintegrated into the consciousness.

This process is usually based on three fundamental goals:

- Becoming aware of our experiences: This is the first step before engaging in mindfulness. You have to decide on what makes you anxious and the experiences that you had in the past that acts as its catalyst. Furthermore, you should observe the internal and external avoidance actions that you have taken to suppress or avoid the emotions attached.
- Develop a more flexible outlook at your situation and circumstances. By all means, you must try to change from having a very critical, rigid and controlling mindset into a more loving, compassionate, nonjudgmental attitude. In other words, have an open mind.
- Improve your quality of life in all areas. You must emphasize cognitive flexibility and live the present rather than being stuck in the past. Doing this will bring about serious changes that will enrich your lives.

You might be wondering why you would ever want to pay attention to a thought that you probably see as your biggest problem. Well, there is no better way to get rid of these anxious thoughts than dealing with them. The more you avoid the thoughts, the more you make yourself a victim of its influence and remain a slave to it, but if you actively look for those thoughts, you will start to notice them as less troubling than before.

Through mindfulness, you will begin to see your thoughts, emotions, and impulses as they are, without allowing them to distract you from achieving your daily goal.

This mindset will help you choose who you should pay attention to, give credit to, and respond more calmly and wisely.

What are the benefits of continuous mindfulness practice?

The following benefits are attached with mindfulness:

- You will be amazed at how much you begin to learn about yourself. You get to tap on inert potentials that your emotions had blinded you from in the past.

- You will enjoy a broaden vision that goes beyond your previous limitations and barriers.

- Your confidence will be boosted to a high level. Those things that would have been a threat in the past now become perfectly normal and lose their power to frighten you and keep you on the edge.

- When you allow it, you will achieve the natural dissolution of all fearful circumstances. This natural dissolution cycle is like that for any living being. Thoughts come before our watchful consciousness, develop and die under the power of our mindfulness.

- The practice of mindfulness enables you to see how your thoughts, emotions, and feelings change rapidly and radically. You will realize that there is no way to maintain or fix "happy" states and permanently rule out "unpleasant" states and so you will be able to live a life devoid of unnecessary worry and panicky.

Chose mindfulness over remaining a perpetual prisoner to your fear

By applying mindfulness as it has been explored in this chapter, we use the same principle as *"exposure and prevention of responses"* often used in cognitive behavioral therapy. We approach what we are afraid of with the boldness of a lion and wait until the anxiety subsides and disappears.

This bold decision to remain unwavering in the face of fear reduces the emotional reaction that would have occurred under an atmosphere of worry and anxiety. The entire human system develops resistance over emotional suffering and is now seen as something less unpleasant and less threatening. This can lead to better tolerance for consequences and adverse situations.

With mindfulness, you can deliberately create a situation that causes anxiety and learn to deal with it. This increases your ability to cope with it. Your new challenge now is to devote enough time to get your desired results.

CHAPTER 3: HOW TO MANAGE THOUGHTS TO CONTROL ANXIETY

When you have an external cut, all you have to do is apply disinfectant to treat it and prevent infection. In time, the wound will close up and you will be as good as new.

How beautiful it will be if you can address negative thoughts and anxiety-provoking thoughts like this! Addressing negative thoughts that control anxiety is not as straightforward.

In addressing negative thought, various approaches can help. The good news is that this manual will shed light on the best ways to deal with your thoughts to prevent it from graduating to anxiety disorder.

One important and helpful way is to make mental shifts. In other words, intentionally adjusting the way you think of challenging an established thought pattern. This happens by changing the way you judge an event or situation. It is a form of training for the brain such that it doesn't succumb to anxiety generating thoughts.

This is not going to be a straightforward process because it involves "uninstalling" and "deprogramming" many negative behaviors and thinking patterns responsible for anxiety. If as a little girl, for instance, your dad keeps hammering it that no one will love you if you are fat, it will end up haunting the girl for life. Hence, she might even resort to unhelpful means to try and keep fit.

A mental shift is one guaranteed way to break off the shackles of unhelpful thoughts. This chapter will shed light on unhelpful thinking patterns and how to manage them to control anxiety.

Beware of thoughts that place excessive demands on you. They start with "I" or "should." Many at times, these demands are impossible to live up to which ends up fueling our anxiety. Consider the following:

Instead of…	Try…
I should wake up early tomorrow	I will sleep early and try to wake up early tomorrow
I should stop eating this kind of food	These food items are not healthy for me. I need to be in good health hence taking… will help
I should make more friends	I need to go out more often, make myself approachable and smile hoping someone will notice and talk to me

The problem with this sort of thought is the compulsion and pressure it puts on us. When this gets to a level, we end up procrastinating or avoiding what we want to do as a means of escaping. In the long run, this ends up triggering more anxiety.

With this in mind, rather than telling yourself you should do things, think of a kind, calm and gentle approach to keep yourself motivated towards the task before you. You can think of another means without graduating into a negative thought pattern.

Understanding Cognitive Distortions

In addition to "Should" form of thinking, other ways negative thoughts express themselves are called cognitive distortions. A few of them are

Mental Filtering

With mental filtering, the victim only concentrates heavily on the negative side of events. In other words, no matter the bright side of an event, he or she does not care. They are so paralyzed by the negativity that they do not celebrate their achievement. They dwell on this till it triggers anxiety.

For instance, take the case of a married couple where the husband cheated. Even after promising and swearing never to repeat such an act of infidelity, the wife will not let go. She even questions all the years of their marriage, thinking and assume it is all a lie.

Black and White Thinking Pattern

Also known as polarized thinking, this person approaches everything with an all or nothing mentality. In other words, humans or circumstances are either perfect or not. They are either the best parent or they are a failure. This affects their relation and disposition to life in general as no middle ground exists in their world. This explains why this person can easily fall to anxiety and negative thinking pattern when things do not go on the positive side.

Overgeneralization

With this distortion, a person concludes (most times, bad) from a single incident. For instance, a person who once had a terrorist attack at a mall will conclude that malls are places where evil lurks. He or she will do all in their capacity to avoid going to the mall. They expect the terrible event to be a norm that should keep repeating at the mall. This person will, in turn, suffer severe anxiety at the thought of visiting the mall.

Another example is a shy guy that summons the courage to talk to a lady he's had feelings for. Assuming his voice failed him in trying to do this, he could conclude that he sucks and will never try to talk to a lady again. Simply entertaining the thought of trying again could send his heart rating triggering anxiety.

Mind reading or Jumping to Conclusion

From the name, people in this category assume to know what everyone is thinking. The issue with this is that their assumption is usually negative which is wrong most times.

For instance, your husband suddenly frowns in the middle of a meal and you conclude he doesn't like the meal or it is salty. This assumption makes you sad triggering anxiety at what could come after. This could, however, be wrong as he could suddenly remember an unpleasant situation that made him uncomfortable.

Personalization

With this distortion, the victim assumes that everything someone else says or does is directly related to them. Everything will be taken personally. As a result, the victim engages in an unhealthy comparison for the best, smartest or brightest.

The sad part is that this person takes the blame for unpleasant things that has no link to them. For instance, 'If I had stayed at home, Tom would have studied for his exam and passed.' This makes the person sink into a pattern of unhealthy thought which could trigger anxiety.

Fallacy of Fairness

In an ideal world, everyone is happy, things go smooth because the world is governed by an unseen rule of right or wrong. Unfortunately, however, this does not happen which could make some people feel bad when confronted with the unpleasant parts of life. This person fails to realize that life is not fair and things will not always go our way.

This person lives life, assuming that everything would be fair. However, when life events and circumstances disobey this rule, the person ends up with negative thoughts which could cause anxiety.

How to Control Negative Thoughts to Beat Anxiety

Every blessed day, humans' battle with unwanted thoughts: "How could I be so stupid?" "I will never learn," "I cannot seem to do anything right," etc. We place such high demands on ourselves and our mind succumb to such negative thoughts. In return, it triggers anxiety, worry, doubt, and feeling of unworthiness. The worst case is that this negative thought makes a cycle that keeps repeating itself over and over.

The good news is that there are many positive steps you can take to have a turnaround and break free of the cycle of thoughts that causes anxiety. You can come up with a viable strategy to counter those thoughts to prevent anxiety. This section explores how you can control negative thoughts:

1. **Turn Negative to Positive Action**

Should you be bewildered with an obsessive thought that's calling you to do something, listen to the dictate of that thought and attend to it. In the same way, you will not ignore the check engine light of your vehicle forever. No matter how hard you try to avoid looking at it, it is right before you every time you are driving. You will not because of the check engine light discard the vehicle or give it out. In the same manner, should thought be a cry for help, do not ignore it.

In other words, take a break and attend to the situation. If you feel scared and tensed to the extent of triggering anxiety, for instance, take a break and consider what is making you scared. Rather than pushing the feeling away, take some time off and examine why you are scared as well as looking for how to address it.

Once you are calm enough to deal with the matter, come up with an action plan. By this, we mean positive and actionable steps that can help. Doing this should address the real source of the anxiety, rather than trying to push the thoughts away.

2. Avoid Indulging in the Level of Futility

In dealing with unhelpful thoughts, there is a tendency to keep doing what doesn't work. However, the problem is evident – they never work. The issue is because of how easy it is easy for the brain to succumb to these useless tactics over and over.

With this in mind, rather than falling back to self-defeating thoughts, consider another approach. It is not about fighting old habits but noticing what doesn't work and sticking to what works.

3. Expand Your Awareness

A constricted mind is like a tight muscle. The degree of movement will be very limited. A few of the things that constrict the mind are old beliefs, inertia, habits, fear, low expectations, and old conditioning. You, however, need to confront this with all honesty.

A closed mindset does no good. With this in mind, on detecting any inner discomfort, be sure to expand your awareness. For instance, a feeling of hatred towards your neighbor is a clear example of a contracted mindset. With an open mindset, however, you can tolerate the person, see another good side of them rather than seeking out their fault.

4. Combat Shades of Green Thinking

Our mind has been conditioned to taking the easy way out. In thinking and making decisions, we love the easy way as it speeds our progress and helps our decision making. This is about dealing with black and white thinking pattern which could be challenging as it holds the person to irrational beliefs.

Rather than getting anxious with shades of gray thought, we recommend evaluating circumstances on a scale of 0 to 10. Falling short of expectations should be seen as a partial failure, rather than sinking into anxiety and beating yourself up.

For instance, someone could say, "I am very useless, I could not wake up to go over my notes for this evening's exam." However, how sure are you that missing a single morning will affect your chance of success? When you analyze this on a scale, it could be a 7% likelihood. This helps removes the anxiety of looking at the circumstance in terms of complete failure.

5. See Disappointments as Part of Life

You might not be able to do much about disappointments. With this in mind, condition your mind to expect them once a while. Avoid thinking too much of people and circumstances so that should things go in a way you didn't like; the blow will not be too much. Life will throw a lot at you. Bear in mind that your reactions to all the happenings have a lot to do in your wellbeing. You can either sink into anxiety or rise above it, seeing it as part of life.

It is vital to know the difference between the things you can control and the ones you cannot. It takes a wise man to let go of things he cannot control. This is the secret to happiness and rising above anxiety that comes with disappointments. You were jilted despite your faithfulness and dedication to the relationship. It hurts, we know, but mourn it and move forward, preparing yourself for the next available partner.

Conclusion

It is often said that thoughts are like birds flying. While you cannot stop these birds from flying, you can stop them from making a nest on your head. In other words, while you might not be able to control thoughts from coming, you can refuse to dwell on them, preventing it from sinking you into a cycle of anxiety and depression.

The good news is that you can take actionable steps to prevent this. The teachings of this chapter have shed light on this.

CHAPTER 4: HOW TO MANAGE ACTIVITIES TO REDUCE ANXIETY

I believe that your journey through this book so far has been a soul-lifting one and you have started applying the anxiety-obliterating techniques you have learned up to this point. I am also certain you are ready to learn more techniques that will help you forget that you ever had an issue with anxiety. In this chapter, you will learn how to properly manage your day to day activities. The techniques are sequential and according to the order of priority so that you can live a fuller and more mentally stable life.

You see, many people find themselves in the middle of activities and don't even know which one to take up first and which one to attend to later. There is always a tendency to do things haphazardly without having a proper plan or time-bound goal and then when everything seems not to be moving as desired, they get overwhelmingly anxious and perplexed.

We indeed live in a busy, fast and anxious world where sitting down to take a pen and paper for the sake of planning seems to appear as a waste of time. Never before in history have people had such a busy and stressful lifestyle as we do now. As a result, we have an astronomical increase in the number of people struggling with different forms of anxiety disorder.

As we go along with our daily activities, it is even difficult to find those who take note of the good things of life around them. These are simple things like beautiful flowers in the squares, sounds of birds singing in the woods or have time to talk about the important events in their lives with loved ones on their balconies. Paradoxically, we are in the age where the entertainment industry is at its best but for many, it is still the most boring part of their lives.

Giving Priority to Importance, Over Urgency

All your daily activities and tasks can be classified into four different groups on the ground of urgency and importance.

- Take the tasks of the first group as both urgent and important.
- Take the tasks of the second group as important, but not urgent.
- Take the tasks of the third group as urgent, but not important.
- Take the tasks of the fourth group as not urgent and not important.

Usually, people begin to work with what is urgent and do not pay any attention to importance, and after so many hours they just continue wallowing in routine and routine work. In the end, they discover they had been busy but their result is as if they had not been doing anything.

"Importance" and "urgency" vary significantly. It all depends on your priorities. You may end up always doing urgent and unimportant things, putting off really important things "for later". Or, by force of will, prioritize "importance" over "urgency", thereby making important matters have more priority over urgent tasks.

In the end, a majority of urgent matters are turnover with minimal efficiency, and the majority of deferred ones are really important matters with high efficiency. This sort of organization technique can only guarantee anxiety and depression.

To increase personal effectiveness, you need to solve problems in this sequence:

- Important and urgent.
- Important and not urgent.
- Not important and urgent.
- Not important and not urgent.

Key Areas to Manage

Properly Manage your Eating

Research has shown that eating habits and the type of food you eat can greatly affect your state of mind. Many nutritionists recommended vegetables like spinach, all citrus fruits, chocolate, meat, fish, egg, banana. This is because they have been medically proven to be rich in nutrients and minerals such as flavonoid, folic acid and vitamin C that reduces anxiety and eases the mind.

Maintaining a good and healthy meal plan where the right food is eaten at the right time will greatly help in reducing anxiety. This must be a conscious decision; you must review what you are eating to know their influence on your mental health.

Keep your work environment organized

There is perhaps nothing more exhausting than working in a disorganized office where you have to spend minutes searching for things. When you look at that table full of papers and you don't even know where to start from, it could be a very frustrating adventure. This, without a doubt, will not help you especially when you are prone to anxiety.

This is why it's crucial to always maintain your work environment, and keep it organized at all times. To get started, set up your table and create a harmonious and welcoming place to develop your ideas.

If your business allows it, decorate your office with beautiful objects and other things that can make you feel good. Photos of your family, some religious symbol, a stone of your sign, incense sticks. Also, add a picture of a place that makes you feel relaxed. Whatever it is, the important thing is the feeling of tranquility. They may seem like small changes, but they are the source of real mental transformation.

Map out your priorities

With a more organized environment, you will be better equipped to take the next step which is setting priorities at your workplace. If you are the type who gets lost amid so many activities, then it is time to plan and organize the tasks that must be accomplished.

When priorities are undefined and everything ends up at the last minute, anxiety becomes even more potent. The tip here is to organize your tasks in an order that makes sense to you.

Another valuable advice is to estimate the time required for each task. This way, you don't overwhelm yourself with excessive tasks.

To have a safe margin to deal with unforeseen events, estimate each period with some surplus. Before starting a new week, take some time to plan the days.

Only set Reasonable and Realistic goals

One of the ways to ensure the success of any given task is to have a clear set of actions and **objectives that are within your ability.** This is because any impossible or unreasonable objectives lead to no result, and continuing to pursue an unattainable objective can cause despair, anger or fear and open the door to anxiety and depression if the goal isn't achieved at the end.

However, a well-planned and prudent goal increases the chances of success and you can anticipate the gratification that awaits you if the goal is achieved.

Manage your sleep and rest time

Make sure you do not deprive yourself of eight hours of sleep every blessed day. This recommendation was made by several national health organizations around the world, which includes the British NHS and the American National Sleep Foundation. Studies conducted around different parts of the world to determine how diseases affect different populations all came to the same conclusion which is: people who suffer from sleep deprivation, just like those who sleep too much, are more susceptible to numerous types of diseases.

As part of good sleep management practice, you must ensure to keep away from anything that can interrupt your sleep. Listening to the television and radio or leaving your mobile phone on when you go to sleep is bad practice. Scroll through your social media feeds at night is also a bad sleep practice so, maximize your sleep time to the advantage of your mental health.

Engage in Exercises

The relationship between physical activity and anxiety has been scientifically established. According to a recent study, both aerobic exercise and strength training reduces anxiety, especially when they are performed regularly. The beneficial effects of exercise are similar to those of meditation.

Exercising regularly can relieve depression and anxiety in the following ways:

- It releases endorphins that generate well-being, natural brain

chemicals that affect similar to cannabis (endogenous cannabinoids) and other natural brain chemicals that can improve your mood.
- It frees the mind from distress and worries which allow you to get out of negative thoughts that help depression and anxiety thrive.

A daily training program lasting for at least 20-30 minutes can significantly reduce anxiety symptoms. Careful consideration of the effects of exercise shows that regular exercise reduces the severity and frequency of anxiety disorders. However, physical exercises cannot be considered as a cure for depression or anxiety but help to improve its symptoms.

You need to do at least 3 or 5 exercise sessions of about 40 minutes long, weekly, starting from low-intensity workouts that can be increased from time to time.

At the end of each activity devote time to rest and catch your breath, at least 20 minutes of breathing and stretching exercises. Drink a lot of water before and after training to help your body stay hydrated. Choose the physical activity that suits you most. Ensure you persevere and are persistent.

Have some fun-time

In 2012, a study carried out in Taiwan, China, showed that adults with less time for pleasure and leisure had more stress-related problems. When a person is anxious, the body will always be on alert, and this means it will constantly keep releasing adrenaline. Leonard Verea, a psychiatrist specializing in psychosomatic medicine and occupational medicine explained that *"A few hours of sleep and leisure serve to reduce levels of this hormone,"*

But what exactly is a fun time? Christian Barbosa, time management and personal productivity expert describes it as *"any time that you create for yourself to take part in activities that you enjoy a lot and make you think creatively,"*

Take short breaks during the day, change position and move.

It may seem difficult, but in a perplexing situation, when you feel that everything is out of control, taking a mental and emotional break is critical.

Create Time to Talk with Loved Ones

When you have close and supportive friends, you will be in a good position to deal with a mental anxiety disorder. This is because, during the time of anxiety, the mind is usually the worst enemy. This is where you need good friends that you can rely on. They can be a shoulder to cry on when anxiety kicks in.

Friends can be very supportive. It could be closed and distant friends. You could communicate via chat or email.

Seek Professional Help if talking to your loved one didn't help

Sometimes, just a friendly shoulder is not enough. If you are in a more advanced state of anxiety, be sure to seek expert help. Seek directions from professionals such as psychologists, psychiatrists, and psychoanalysts. They have the resources, knowledge, and techniques to help you understand how to contain anxiety, manage and gradually recover.

With the support of these people, you have the opportunity to face the problem head-on and find increasingly efficient mechanisms to deal with situations that are bad for you. Do not hesitate and do not feel embarrassed: you are responsible for your well-being and need to watch over it.

Go in search of the moments of happiness that you have lost due to the stressful situations you experience with the assistance of a professional.

CHAPTER 5: WAYS TO FIND INSTANT CALM AND OVERCOME ANXIETY

"Between stimulus and response, there is a space. In that space is our power to choose our response. In our response lies our growth and our freedom." ~Victor Frankl

The above sums up how we can deal with anxiety. Even though we have no control over anxiety stimulus and the things that make us nervous, we can control how we react. Anxiety thrives when we fuel it, telling ourselves that we are helpless in times of dreadful situations.

We feed on this lie, which in turn makes us afraid, lost and helpless. We become paralyzed as if we are under the grip of some unseen forces that are out to snuff life out of us. It is like we are lost in the ocean, amidst shark, whales and other scary sea animals.

We imagine the worst as our imagination lights up with horrible things that can happen. This is the grip of anxiety on many people. To make matters worse, we wrongly assume that we are helpless, hence we succumb to the all the nightmares and thoughts of everything that can go wrong. The truth, however, is that we can control this.

We have all been there. I, for instance, have had my fair share of horrible times. Life has come knocking hard on me. I have lost thousands of dollars in investment, dealt with job loss, had my fair share of relationship failure and fought for my health.

I, however, have some formula that worked for me to bring me calm in a distressing situation. No matter what I am going through, anytime, anywhere, I can apply these techniques and drift into a state of tranquility.

We are presenting easy and simple techniques that you can remember any time which has a soothing effect on your mind and body. The best part is when your imaginations start acting up, you can activate them to bring instant calm.

1. **Freeze Yourself**

When we were kids, one of my favorite games involved freezing where you stopped suddenly, irrespective of what you are doing. It happens the same ways fish and other aquatic lives are frozen in the cold room. The idea is to apply this to your body parts, emotions and thought process.

Freeze yourself for a couple of seconds and watch how the anxiety and tension evaporates. Better still; imagine yourself as an alien that was hit with a stun gun.

2. **Bring Yourself Back to the Moment**

Many times when we are anxious, it is because of something we have no power over. It is because of something in the future. Rather than disturbing yourself on what will happen and imagining all possible worse case scenarios, bring yourself back to the moment.

One helpful tactic is to ask yourself what is happening at the moment? Is your life under attack? Are you facing a life or death situation? Can you do anything about what is getting you worked up? If not, concentrate on the moment and check-in with those thoughts later.

3. Re-label What is Happening

Have you seen someone having a panic attack? Usually, it feels like they are under the grip of a certain force with which they have no control. To other people, they even feel like they are dying. Yet, careful observation of the fact shows that the present situation is completely harmless and temporary.

Bear in mind that your body, during the process has just activated the flight or fight hormones which got you all worked up. This is meant to keep you alive, and not snuff life out of you as you might assume.

4. Fact-Check Your Thoughts

One of the reasons anxiety is bad is because people fixate on the worst scenario. You are imagining every possible thing that can go wrong. This, in turn, is sending your hormones haywire. For instance, you are about talking to a lady you have a soft spot for.

As you are about to approach her, you can feel your heart racing like it will jump off your chest. Rather than think you are going to make a fool of yourself, tell yourself you are going to give it your best. Besides, the worst-case scenario is for her to reject you. The heavens will not come crashing down either will she beat you up. The realization that the worst scenarios are not as bad as our imagination paints it can help.

With this in mind, form a habit of examining and fact-checking your fears. With this, your brain can relate to anxious thoughts normally rather than acting up.

5. Take deep breaths

In the heat of battle, when bullets are flying around, one of the relaxation techniques used by soldiers in combat is deep breaths. This is due to the calming effect it has on the muscles. It is not about counting some numbers. The idea is inhaling and exhaling evenly. It works wonders by bringing your attention to the present and slowing down your mind. With this, you can focus and rise above the nervousness that plagues you.

6. Stand Up Straight

In times of anxiety, it is normal for us to try and protect our upper body parts. It is an instinct since this is where our vital organs are located. As a result, many people end up hunching over when anxiety kicks in.

To combat this physical reaction, try and stand up straight, walk around with your shoulders pulled back. Open your chest and pull your feet apart. The idea is signaling to your body that you are in charge and there is no imminent danger. Do this, rather than curling up on your couch or burying your head, lost in thoughts.

7. Focus on Your Index Finger

For the next fifteen to sixty seconds, concentrate on your index finger. Let your mind and body be consumed by it.

Feel it, bring it nearer, caress it, and examine the creases, rivets and the fingerprints. This simple mindfulness action can bring your thought back to reality and the consciousness of what is happening around you.

8. Look around You Mindfully

Anxiety attacks us because we get lost in thoughts. However, one helpful way is to mindfully bring ourselves to the environment. The key is mindfully noticing everything around you. As you do this, consciously notice the thoughts that are crippling into your head trying to distract you.

This feeling brings you in touch with the self and the immediate environment. It helps you connect with the moment. By doing this, you can recognize that the root of your discomfort is your thoughts. This is where the troubling emotions start.

9. Watch a Funny Video

This is my favorite after a hard day's job. Watching comedy is a way of distracting yourself and forgetting your worries. When you laugh, it eases your anxious mind and calms your muscles. Without any doubt, there are many benefits of laughter to the health – both physical and mental. It can reduce anxiety the same way exercise does.

In addition to the recommended techniques above, you can also try some Pranayama exercises to find instant calm. More of these discussed below:

Simple Pranayama Exercises for Instant Calm

Pranayama teaches people to control their breath to bring about enlightenment, purification, and relaxation. It brings superb calmness that can help you calm the mind. Some of them are discussed below:

i. Nadi Shodhana Breath

If you are looking for quick relief from stress and anxiety, try this technique that is also called "alternate nostril breathing." It helps in bringing balance to the two hemispheres of the brain. We explain how to do this below:

- Get a comfortable sitting position
- Bring your right hand up to your face

- With your right thumb, close your right nostril
- Breath in gently through your left nostril
- After inhaling, pause for some seconds
- With your ring finger, close the left nostril
- Through the right nostril, let out the breath
- Keep this up for a couple of minutes

Be sure to be fully engaged in the practice as you bring balance to the brain. If you find that you are unable to calm down after a long day, you can use this alternate nostril breathing technique. With it, you can calm your mind and enjoy a peaceful sleep.

ii.   Sahita Kumbhaka Breath

Breathing is a natural process for man. As a result, we go about breathing in and out without much thought into the little moment that exists between breathing in and out. That little moment between breaths is called kumbhaka and helps us find calmness. You can practice this by:

- Slowly inhaling
- At the top of the breath, pause and hold it for a few moments
- Slowly let out the air
- Once the last ounce of air is expelled, hold it for a moment
- Repeat this for a couple of minutes before returning to your normal breathing routine.

Without a doubt, this is an unnatural breathing pattern and could feel weird. This is expected since we go about our day by day activities mindlessly. In time, however, you will find this breathing pattern helpful alongside the calmness effect on anxiety. This will lead you to a steady, deep, intentional breath in time.

iii. Ujjayi Breath

If you are looking to cool your body and nervous system, you can try this wonderful pranayama practice. We recommend settling down in a place without distraction as you try this breathing technique. The following explains how to go about it:

- Get a comfortable sitting position and keep your back straight.
- With your nose, breathe in and out.
- Breathe firmly and exhale the air using the back of your nasal passage.
- Be sure to relax and repeat the process for a couple of minutes.
- The highlight of this practice is to have your breath in a rhythm, like that of an ocean wave.

This is best done alongside your yoga practice. However, when faced with mental strain, anxiety, and nervousness, you can employ this to bring calmness to your mind.

CHAPTER 6: MEDICATIONS AND HERBS TO TREAT ANXIETY

Many people experience anxiety and panic attacks with symptoms like sweating, chest tightness and a loss of control. Anxiety is overwhelming and scary and can wreak havoc on one's life.

The symptoms of anxiety differ and can range from long to short term. The signs differ for various people. Someone could get all worked up for something as simple as meeting someone for the first time. Someone else could be restless all because she has to clean the house.

Signs of anxiety are both physical and psychological with symptoms that can be mild or annoying as in the case of a panic attack. Whatever your symptoms, looking for a healthy coping mechanism that works for you is important.

Constant living under fear, anxiety, and tension can be hazardous to one's life. The symptoms could be so overwhelming that the victim might crave instant relief. This is why this chapter will shed light on medications that can help with anxiety and all its form. In addition to these medications, we will explore natural remedies, herbs, and supplements to help fight anxiety.

Herbs to Fight Anxiety

Find below a list of helpful herbs to put anxiety under control

1. **Valerian Root**

One of the effects of anxiety that many people suffer is insomnia. With valerian root, you can reduce insomnia and get a deep, relaxing and restful sleep. Besides helping to induce sleep, it is a completely natural remedy. Taken in pill form, it helps the body relax. It has been used for centuries by the Greeks and Romans as a natural remedy for anxiety.

2. **Kava Kava**

Available in various forms, this is a well-known remedy for anxiety which promotes relaxation. Even though a natural herb, it is available in the pill form. It has a soothing effect on the body, it helps relax the muscles and improves mental ability.

According to many research, kava kava is a safe treatment for anxiety without any side effects. As a precaution though, it is best not to take kava with alcohol due to the negative interaction. In suppressing anxiety, however, alcohol is not recommended.

3. **Ashwagandha**

This is a natural herb that is translated "smell of horse." For ages, it has been used to treat anxiety, low energy and to fight aging. It is common in Ayurvedic medical practice. It is an adaptogenic herb with natural healing capacity that helps balance, restore and protect the body.

Ashwagandha helps restore balance to the hormone responsible for anxiety. In addition to this, it induces sleep and helps the body relax. It also has a soothing effect on cortisol, the stress hormone that triggers anxiety.

4. Lavender

Lavender is used widely in aromatherapy as the plant comes with essential oil that triggers relaxation in anxiety victims. It comes in essential oil, and also available in pill form. Lavender has been used widely to create instant calm in tensed and anxious people. It is a beautiful and fragrant plant that helps improves mood and reduces anxiety. It has a smoothening effect on both chronic and mild anxiety

One of the things that suffer as a result of anxiety is sleep. Lavender induces deep and restful sleep in victims. You can improve your sleep quality simply by using lavender pillow spray or having a pot of lavender in your room. You can also use it in a bath or with few drops applied which can help relax symptoms. Lavender is gentle and relaxing and can be taken in tea.

With cases of extreme anxiety, you might have a small bottle of lavender oil in your bag. It can be used externally, especially for pregnant women.

5. Passionflower

This is a beautiful flower that has been of help to many anxiety sufferers. It calms the nerves and hormones, making anxiety lose their grip on victims. We recommend taking passionflower later in the evening as it induces sleep in people, especially after a busy day.

Passionflower has been used and accepted all over the world as a treatment for anxiety. Some species of the plant also help in treating stomach upset.

6. Chamomile

A sip of chamomile tea before bed might just be your ticket to a good night's sleep. If you do not like tea, chamomile is also available in pill form. It is an anxiety herb that is gentle, effective and provides a soothing effect on anxiety. It encourages sleep, eases digestion and pretty effective in combat insomnia. It is a herb approved in European Countries. It is safe for use during pregnancy and breastfeeding.

You can combine chamomile with lemon balm herbal tea. Lemon balm is recommended for producing an instant calming effect which can help reduce anxiety.

7. Lemon Balm

Traditionally known as gladdening herb, lemon balm has been a common herb, widely accepted in Western Europe. It is a known herb that helps bring about a sense of calm, decreasing anxiety and lightening one's spirit. It can be combined with lavender tea and chamomile.

We recommend using lemon balm in the evening because it reduces alertness and produces a mild sensation. As a result, you are better off using the lemon balm on your day off and evening rather than before an exam. It comes in capsule form even though an extract. It also helps treat digestive issues and headaches.

8. Reishi Mushroom

This is in the class of herbs known as adaptogens – the class of herbs that comes in handy in adapting to the stress and demands of everyday life without succumbing to the anxiety and pressure that comes along. They come with potent tonic action that helps regulate and manage the body's stress response.

Reishi mushroom is a medicinal mushroom that produces a calm, soothing and relaxing effect on people with anxiety. It is one of the best adaptogens to deal with anxiety, helping to relax the muscles for good night sleep. It is safe to use while breastfeeding.

9. Tumeric or Curcumin

Not only does turmeric work for digestion and inflammation, but it has also been shown to be of great benefit in treating anxiety and depression. It is a root plant called rhizome rich in a compound called phytochemicals' potent for reversing inflammation.

There are specific anxieties that are linked to the chronically activated stress response. The curcumin in turmeric comes with strong anti-inflammatory effects which helps to combat such chronic anxiety. In powdered form, you can add it to food, and smoothies which can help heal the digestive system.

Turmeric is safe to use as a spice for seasoning. It is safe for use in pregnancy and while breastfeeding. We recommend taking the curcumin extracts for the anti-anxiety effect.

Concluding Herbs for Anxiety

We recommend talking to your health practitioner before resorting to any of this herb. The good news is that since these are natural herbs, there is no side effect of any form. You can break free of the shackles of anxiety and tension that is holding you back.

The next section explores common and potent medications that can help deal with anxiety.

Anxiety Medications

Be sure to talk to your doctor before trying out any medication for anxiety. This is important to ensure that you are fit for the medication. Also, it is important to prepare for the side effects that will be discussed. All in all, be careful not to depend solely on medication as it does not produce a permanent fix but a temporary relieve.

With the above in mind, here are potent drugs that can help with anxiety.

Benzodiazepines

These are sedatives widely known for their calming effect on the muscle and mind. Thy target some neurotransmitters (chemicals that relay messages between the brain cells) and increase their effectiveness. They have been known to treat many forms of anxiety-like social anxiety disorder, panic attacks, and generalized anxiety disorder. Some drugs in this category are:

- lorazepam (Ativan)
- alprazolam (Xanax)
- diazepam (Valium)
- chlordiazepoxide (Librium)
- clonazepam (Klonopin)

These classes of drugs are pretty effective in providing instant relief for anxiety treatment. They increase drowsiness, making victims drift off thereby escaping the grip of anxiety. We recommend taking benzodiazepines only on doctor's prescription as they come with side effects such as memory problems, drowsiness, headaches, and vision problem. Also, if you have been on benzodiazepines medication for more than two weeks, we advise that you not stop the drug suddenly as it can bring about withdrawal symptoms like seizures. Talk to your doctor to help reduce the dosage until you can safely stop it.

Buspirone

Buspirone affects chemicals in the brain that controls mood. It is pretty effective in combating long and short term anxiety. For maximum effectiveness, the buspirone needs to be taken for many weeks. It comes with side effects like nausea, headaches or difficulty sleeping.

Antidepressants

Effective in addressing anxiety symptoms, antidepressant medications react majorly on the neurotransmitters. However, you need to be consistent with them for a month before recording any reasonable effect. There are many forms of antidepressant; we discuss some of them below

Selective Serotonin Reuptake Inhibitors

Also known as SSRIs, they increase the serotonin levels of the body. Serotonin is a neurotransmitter in charge of appetite, mood, sexual desire, memory, and sleep. Selective serotonin reuptake inhibitors used in treating anxiety come in many forms. Examples are:

- sertraline (Zoloft)
- escitalopram (Lexapro)
- fluoxetine (Prozac)

Be sure to only take SSRIs based on the prescription of the doctor as they come with side effects. Common side effects are diarrhea, dizziness, sexual dysfunction, dry mouth, and muscle weakness.

Tricyclics

Tricyclics are also selective serotonin reuptake inhibitors that treat many forms of anxiety disorders except for obsessive-compulsive disorder (OCD). Common examples are clomipramine (Anafranil) and imipramine (Tofranil). The use of tricyclics has reduced as newer drugs with mild side effects have been developed.

With tricyclics, expect side effects like dry mouth, dizziness, constipation, blurred vision, low energy levels, etc.

Supplements to Control Anxiety

In addition to medications and herbs, some supplements can help reduce anxieties and their symptoms. Bear in mind, however, that supplements should not stand in place of other therapies to treat anxiety. They should only be used as an addition to support your treatment effort.

Generally, supplements do not pose any problem to the body. However, the effect on the body might differ. This is due to age, pregnancy, and any other health conditions. Also, some supplements pose a health problem when taken in excessive doses.

All in all, be sure to inform your doctor before going for any supplements. They are in the best position to advise you on potential side effects and any other effect the drug might have on you. Also, bear in mind that you might not need these supplements if you are feeding on a balanced diet. With a diet lacking essential nutrients, however, these supplements can help keep anxiety at bay.

Magnesium

Magnesium is a supplement with a powerful calming effect on the central nervous system. This helps prevents nervousness, restlessness, irritability, fear, and anxiety. Magnesium protects the heart, making it all the more helpful if you suffer from panic attacks

You can take 400 to 600 mg of magnesium per day in supplements. It is typically taken with calcium (800 to 1200 mg). You can take magnesium and calcium supplement at night for deep and restful sleep. You can increase your magnesium intake by bathing with a cup of Epsom salt in warm water. This can be spiced up with lavender essential oil.

You can improve your intake of magnesium by focusing on spinach, kale, leafy vegetables, millets, oats, etc.

Vitamin D

This is a fat-soluble vitamin abundant in eggs and other fatty fish like mackerel and cod liver oil. The body makes vitamin D on exposure to the early morning sun. The nutrients from vitamin D can help suppress a feeling of anxiety.

Not only does it help with anxiety, but vitamin D also gives improved bone health, boosts immunity and protects the heart. In supplement form, vitamin D is common in the synthetic form as vitamin D3 (cholecalciferol). Vitamin D2 (ergocalciferol). Natural sourced of vitamin D include salmon and sardines. Fish oil (EPA and DHA) contains omega-3s known to help combat depression and anxiety.

In conclusion

Anxiety is bad and destructive. It can corrupt your day and hold you back from enjoying life to the fullest. This is why finding a way to deal with anxiety is important. We have provided medications; supplements and herbs that can help reduce the symptoms of anxiety.

In using these herbs and medications, be sure to remember that individuals are different with distinct body composition. As a result, the body might react differently.

The next chapter talks about the impact of aromatherapy and acupuncture on addressing anxiety.

CHAPTER 7: AROMATHERAPY AND ACUPUNCTURE

Introducing Aromatherapy

Aromatherapy employs extracts from plants knows as an essential oil to bring improvement to health problems and anxiety. This treatment is administered either by breathing in through the nose or putting them on the skin. It can be used to bath or alongside a massage.

Essential Oils are gotten from herbs, flowers, herbs and tree parts (roots, petals, bark, and peels.) In these plants are cells called "essence" responsible for the fragrance.

True essential oils are unique, and not diluted with any other product (chemicals or fragrance). The process of extracting the fragrance doesn't change the chemical composition of the plant. Some common examples of essential oils are lavender, bergamot, lemon and chamomile

How does Aromatherapy work?

Aromatherapy activates the smell receptors in the nose which engages the brain and nervous system. The oil triggers some parts of the brain like the limbic system which is in charge of emotions. It also affects the hypothalamus. In turn, you have serotonin and other feel-good brain chemicals.

When an essential oil is applied to the skin as well, they activate a certain reaction in the skin and some parts of the body like the joint. Aromatherapy is of great help in easing the symptoms of anxiety. However, aromatherapy should not replace regular treatment for anxiety. In addition to easing stress and anxiety, it encourages relaxation and improves sleep.

Is Aromatherapy Safe?

Generally, as long as you follow the prescription of the doctor, aromatherapy is safe. Although, there could be some side effects like skin and eye irritation and activation of mucus. They could also trigger a mild allergic reaction in people. Aromatherapy is meant for external use only. Drinking might hurt the liver or kidney.

Be sure to work hand in hand with an aromatherapist or your doctor before using any of the recommended essential oils

How to Make Use Essential Oils?

There are many ways to make use of essential oils. These are:

- Inhalation: You can have some drops of the essential oil on your handkerchief and keep with you. You can also use an aromatherapy necklace or bracelet.
- In Your Home: With the use of a diffuser, you can use aromatherapy in your home. You can also use an oil burner

- Massage: Essential oils are also used with oil for massage therapy. If you want to use it yourself, make sure to dilute the oil with a carrier oil (like sweet almond oil). In general, we recommend using just five drops of essential oils with 10 ml of carrier oil.
- Bath: essential oil can be added to your tub water. Just six drops of your desired essential oil added to the running water can help you have a relaxing bath.

Common Example of Essential Oils

For donkey years, essential oils have been used to relieve anxiety. They have an extremely incredible smell and can help with mild or severe anxiety. Essential oils are pretty concentrated for instance a single pound of lavender oil comes from 220 pounds of lavender flower. Common examples are:

Lavender Oil: This is one of the most popular essential oils. It comes with an amazing scent that has a soothing effect on anxiety and stress. It also helps improve sleep.

Rose Oil: Inhaling rose oil brings instant calm to the nerves and eases away tension. If your anxiety comes from grieve, rose oil is good.

Vetiver Oil: Also known as the oil of tranquility, it is popular in Sri Lanka and India. It comes with a sweet, smoky scent. It can help relieve the symptoms of anxiety, panic attack, and depression.

Ylang Ylang Oil: This amazing essential oil comes with a tropical, calming scent. It can help boost emotional wellbeing and also reduces blood pressure. It has a calming effect on anxiety as it comes with mild sedative qualities.

Frankincense Oil: Coming with a fantastic rich aroma, frankincense increases oxygen supply to the brain thereby improving mood and engaging the limbic system. It is best used with the bathwater as it relaxes the joint, the whole body and mind

Geranium Oil: Like a beautiful rose-like smell, geranium oil has a soothing effect such that it helps get rid of negative thoughts. It also has a restoration effect on the hormones.

Basil Essential Oil: It is one of the principal herbs used in India to reduce anxiety and improve mood. It is one of the best essential oil that produces a soothing effect on the central nervous system. It curbs anxiety, reduces fatigue and fights depression. It is a natural stimulant that brings about peace and mind clarity.

Jasmine Oil: For centuries, jasmine oil has been pretty helpful in relieving symptoms of anxiety and depression. It has a calming effect on the nervous system, engaging the brain and improving mood.

Chamomile Oil: With an herby aroma, chamomile oil has a soothing effect on the body when inhaled. It calms anxiety and headache. You can either breathe it in or use it as a massage. When combined with a carrier oil, it can be applied to the belly button and solar plexus.

Bergamot Essential Oil: is made when citrus fruit is peeled. Used by the native Chinese, it enhances the flow of energy, boosts digestion and fights bacteria. It enhances mood, helps against depression and enhances the feeling of joy. It improves blood circulation bringing balance to the body.

Melissa Essential Oil: Famous for its calming, medicinal and uplifting qualities, Melissa oil has been used for centuries. It has a soothing effect on the mind and also strengthens the nervous system. It can help let go of feelings of anxiety, sadness, worry, and depression. You can massage it directly or use it with a warm bath.

Other examples of essential oils and what they treat are:
- Basil: nervine panic, depression, and for nervous tension,
- Geranium: for anxiety, nervine, depression
- Grapefruit: is recommended for addressing depression
- Mandarin: sedative, for anxiety, depression
- Rosewood: for depression
- Marjoram: is a sedative recommended for nervine, and insomnia.
- Rosemary: for depression
- Peppermint: is used for nervine, depression and panic
- Rose: is a sedative, used for nervous tension, self-esteem, and depression
- Sandalwood: is also a sedative, used for nervous tension, anxiety, insomnia, depression
- Neroli: sedative, for anxiety, panic, insomnia, self-esteem, depression
- Sage: is used for depression

Safety Tips with Essential oils

Bear in mind that essential oils come in concentrated form. As a result, it is essential to be safety conscious when using them. When used within the right and recommended a dosage, there is nothing to worry about for adults. You, however, need to be smart and careful when using with babies, in pregnancy, and for children. People with certain medical issues also need to proceed with caution.

For instance, citrus essential oil produces phototoxicity when applied to the skin. When applied and exposed to direct sunlight, it causes sunburn. With this in mind, it is best to use citrus oil at night.

Also, if you want to apply essential oil to the skin, be sure to dilute it with a carrier oil.

What is Acupuncture?

Indigenous to the native Chinese, acupuncture is a healing technique that has existed thousands of years ago. It is based on the fact that when there is an imbalance of energy in the body, it creates mental health conditions. According to traditional Chinese medicine, there are important life energy points in the body called chi. A normal functioning mind and body facilitates a natural flow of the body's energy levels. These channels, known as meridians are located at specific points in the body. There are times these points become congested which cause disorders

With acupuncture, you can bring back health and balance to these blocked channels. The treatment sections involve using small needles at certain places in the body known as acupuncture points. They are the places where the energy blockage occurs.

Acupuncture and Anxiety Treatment

Be sure to get in touch with a licensed acupuncturist to help treat your anxiety. According to research, acupuncture produces a calming effect on anxiety disorder. When compared with the standard treatment plan, it reduces stress, depression and eases tension.

The traditional Chinese medicine (TCM) categorizes some part of the body as Zang and fu. There are five zang in the body (the spleen, the heart, the kidney the lung, and the liver). There are six fu organs as well are: (the urinary bladder, stomach, large intestine, the san jiao the small intestine, and the gall bladder – three areas of the body cavity).

TCM believes that there is a specific role the Zang organs play when it comes to emotions. In other words, the emotions and the organ's health are linked. However, these Zang organs could develop imbalance because of bad lifestyle, hereditary factors, and poor diet. For instance

- Spleen disorder manifests as too much mental work, worry, tension, obsession, etc.
- Liver disorder manifest as anger, frustration, resentment, bitterness, and irritability
- Lung disorder shows itself as grief, detachment, and sadness
- Kidney imbalance is seen through weak willpower, a fearful and insecure person, etc.
- When a person develops anxiety, the spleen is mostly affected, as well as the heart.

Acupuncture comes as a treatment plan to create harmony between the body, emotions, spirit, and mind. The acupuncturist is skilled to discern any imbalance by observing the skin tone, eye color, gait, demeanor, posture voice, palpitation, etc.

According to Traditional Chinese Medicine, health goes hand in hand with Qi (energy). A normal functioning Qi in good health ensures a perfect, smooth and unblocked movement through various channels in the body. Emotions like stress, anger, anxiety, etc. block the free flow of Qi. This explains why people that are stressed complain of neck, shoulder or back pain. This is due to the tensions that are triggered by stresses in these parts.

Acupuncture involves putting needles in various specific points on these channels. Doing this stimulates the body's energy which helps the body heal and restores balance. This is why acupuncture point helps maintain a smooth flow of energy thereby relieving anxiety and stress.

To further help an anxiety sufferer, we recommend positive changes to lifestyle. Tai Chi and yoga are examples of mind-body exercise that helps control anxiety. In controlling anxiety as well, diet is important. Excess intake of carbs and refined sugar, for instance, spikes insulin and blood sugar level. This, in turn, affects the mood. When there is too much caffeine in the body, it creates in the liver, a "toxic heat" which fuels anxiety.

To deal with anxiety and stress, we recommend foods low on the glycemic index. These, alongside acupuncture treatment, will bring about positive change. Since every individual is unique with a distinct set of imbalance, treatment for anxiety using acupuncture also differs.

- Acupuncture helps reduce stress by helping the brain release endorphin – a pain-killing chemical.
- It improves blood circulation the body which gets rid of cortisol (stress hormones) and ensures tissue cells get enough oxygen.
- Acupuncture relaxes the muscle, calms the heart rate and reduces blood pressure.

Without any doubt, acupuncture is safe and free of side effects if done with a trained and licensed acupuncturist. It even brings about the immediate result in some cases, although some might see changes by the following day. This is helpful to people with severe anxiety that needs immediate relief. Acupuncture is effective as it gets to the root of anxiety and eradicates the symptoms. It is suitable to use in all age and safe even in pregnancy.

Why Should You Consider Acupuncture for Anxiety Disorder?

1. Acupuncture is pretty straightforward

As long as you are with a well trained and licensed acupuncturist, the process is straightforward without any complication. The acupuncturist will observe your tongue shape, eye color. He could also ask for your health history and feel your pulse.

After the examination, he will go for a treatment plan to address your health condition. He will check and stimulate various specific acupoints in the body.

Acupuncture produces no pain or discomfort in many cases as it uses fine needles placed at specific points. The needles are placed for about half an hour and removed.

2. Acupuncture treats every patient as Unique

Many victims of anxiety find instant calm using acupuncture. It involves no medication hence consider every patient as a unique entity before administering a treatment that provides a lasting result.

Unlike medications, acupuncture approaches every victim distinctly. Think of it, what causes anxiety in people differ. The acupuncturist first identifies this rather than going directly to address the symptoms. Acupuncture works with the belief that the body and mind are linked hence it involves a treatment that encompasses the entire system.

3. Acupuncture Increases Energy Levels

Demands of everyday life and going about our business and activities lead to stress and reduce our energy levels. This leads to frustration, reduced energy levels which cause moodiness, triggering stress and depression along the line.

With acupuncture, you can support and reenergize your body. By working on our energy points, it helps boosts energy levels. When acupuncture is combined with blood nourishing foods, it can be of great help. Sample blood nourishing foods are the egg, spinach, figs, kale, beetroot, etc.

4. Acupuncture Relaxes the Body

Without a doubt, acupuncture is relaxing and helps relieve stress and anxiety. Many people have recorded instant relieve from stress and anxiety after the treatment.

Even though the idea of needles piercing the body could be overwhelming, it helps foster relaxation. Many people experience so much calm that they drift off while getting treated. With this, it is evident that acupuncture releases stress and helps the body return to normal, without the influence of anxiety and stress.

5. Acupuncture is a Drug-free Treatment

In using medications to address stress and anxiety, there is bound to be a side effect and other discomforts. Acupuncture, on the other hand, is safe, eases pain and other medical condition without side effects.

According to research in Georgetown, it was discovered that acupuncture produces the same effect as anti-depressant and anxiety drugs. When combined with other treatments as well, it can help reduce side effects.

6. Healing Result

Usually, the time taken to see the positive result is a factor of the client and how strong their symptom is. The good news, however, is that many patients experience relief after a single section of acupuncture. For others, it could be the following morning, after a week or even months.

Depending on the patients, acupuncture begins with one or two sections. However, it is a good idea to seek other treatment options if there is no improvement.

Acupuncture Conclusion

Acupuncture is an effective treatment that can provide instant healing for anxiety. If done with an experienced acupuncturist, there can be instant relief without any side effects. It comes with amazing health benefits, improves sleep and generates a stronger sense of control.

Be sure to try acupuncture with your current treatment plan if you are seeking help for anxiety disorder. Opening up to your acupuncturist will help explore a potent treatment plan to get your anxiety under control.

CHAPTER 8: BEHAVIORAL THERAPY FOR ANXIETY DISORDERS

Phobia, one of the most common anxiety disorders is usually learned through paired association and cemented through avoidance and escape. In other words, anything that can be learned via this means could be unlearned. This is the principle of exposure and response prevention therapy – types of behavioral therapy used in controlling anxiety. There are anxiety disorders that can be treated when exposure and response prevention are used.

By exposure, we mean confronting the source of fear or anxiety till it has no power to trigger fear in the victim. Response prevention, on the other, means doing away with escape and avoidance behaviors that usually spring up in the presence of a dreaded situation. This is important for controlling anxiety and other maladaptive behaviors.

Exposure therapy

Exposure therapy uses a phenomenon known as habituation. Habituation is the process in which someone's sensory response and behavioral attitude reduce with time after exposure to certain stimuli. It is a phenomenon common to everyone. It is like bathing with warm water. Simply touching the water, you feel it is probably too hot. However, after pouring the first two or three bowls on your body, you no longer think it's too hot. This means your body has habituated to the water temperature. In the same manner, assuming you are coming from the hot sun, you will probably feel uncomfortable getting to a shed. But in time, your body will adjust to the temperature of the surrounding. This is habituation.

We can apply exposure therapy using Vivo exposure – real exposure to the source of dread. This exposure might be via imagination or both. Imagination is, however, particularly helpful when real exposure is not practical. Imagination is only effective when all five senses are engaged in the exercise. The idea is the same, whether using real or imagined exposure. The aim is to make the victim face the object of dread until habituation occurs when there is no more harm. In time, they no longer have a distressing reaction.

When habituation sets in, anxiety that comes as a result of exposure to the dreaded object disappears. The research revealed that people learn to dread neutral stimuli (needles, snakes, closed places) because they associate it with fear. When we, however, reverse the process, the dreadful behavior will die down gradually. With this in mind, unlearning and un-pairing holds the key to getting rid of anxiety. For instance, a person with claustrophobia (fear of enclosed places) will avoid closed places and associate it with evil. However, if this person is repeatedly exposed to enclosed places, the person can then realize that evil does not lurk in enclosed places. In time, the fear will die down.

Systematic desensitization

By exposure therapy, we introduce and allow people to get comfortable in a fearful situation. This is one of the best treatments for anxiety. However, without a doubt, many people find it difficult to agree with this method. This is where exposure therapy comes in –a variant form of exposure that is less intense. It starts by teaching people relaxation techniques to calm their nerves in a dreadful situation.

Once relaxation becomes part of them, they are exposed gradually to their object of dread in a progressive manner. This exposure might be real or imagined. For instance, for someone with an extreme fear of enclosed places, the person might first be exposed to caves and other enclosed places while practicing the relaxation technique.

In time, they will also ask them to relax while imagining themselves in closed places. Once they get comfortable with this, they can practice the relaxation technique as they try to get in a cave, an elevator or any available enclosed space. In time, they might be able to walk in the cave with someone for as long as it takes to get rid of the fear. This gradual, controlled and systematic approach allows them to become desensitized to their object of dread.

Response Prevention

In addition to exposure therapy, we have response prevention therapy which involves trying to discourage and prevent all forms of maladaptive coping responses like escape and avoidance. For any anxiety disorder treatment to be effective, exposure and response prevention is pretty important.

In the past, it was believed that once someone establishes a memory, the memory is permanent. In time, however, researchers discovered that memories are not always permanent. In contrast, like information on a computer, memory can be edited, changed and even deleted in the right circumstance. This process is known as "memory reconsolidation" in which we "edit" memories that have been established. "Memory consolidation" means the process of establishing a memory. Thanks to research, humans can now manipulate the reconsolidation therapy.

This therapy is pretty promising and useful in getting rid of emotional memories responsible for anxiety disorder. However, what if you need an instant calm from a troubling memory? What if anxiety comes knocking so hard that you need to snap out real quick? The next section shed light on this

Instant Calming Techniques for Anxiety

The survival of humans in their environment depends on how their needs are met. Humans have innate needs with instinct desire to fulfill these needs. For instance, all humans need clothing. Should these needs not be met, we suffer. This is why we need to take action that helps meet our needs. When we take action to balance up our needs, our suffering reduces.

For instance, when you go hungry, it is a clear signal that you are not meeting a need to eat. In the same manner, anxiety is a clear signal that something is lacking – there is a need left unfulfilled.

The link between thoughts and Feelings

Thoughts trigger strong emotions not the other way round. With this in mind, changing feelings appear to be more effective than changing thoughts. Emotions are a basic part of man that is essential to our survival. Here, we discuss three effective techniques with an emphasis on the thinking part of a man to help him gain control.

i.   Concentrate on How feelings Change

Without a doubt, feelings are not constant and are subject to change. Hence, even after your effort to relax and calm your anxiety, you find yourself getting anxious; the best approach is to think about how good you will feel when the feelings die down.

To make this effective, we recommend writing the changes you expect down. If you are to have a thesis defense, you might write something like this down: "I am feeling all tensed up which is expected. I will expect this feeling to change soon in which I will be calm and collected."

In addition to this, we recommend that people imagine how they will feel once they get the change they expect. In other words, the young chap preparing for a thesis defense will be able to speak fluently without mincing words. We recommend you write this down as well.

The overall theme of this first point is that feelings change. Hence, when you feel tensed, remembering this can be pretty effective. When this happens, shift your mind to how good you expect to feel when the nervousness and anxiety disappear.

ii.   Act Normal and Chew it over

In the early course of this book, we established that anxiety, in a specific dose is normal. It was primal to the survival of our ancestors then. The sad part is that this survival instinct can go wrong and serve as a hindrance rather than help us.

There are fierce guard dogs that are so brutal that they do not mind biting off the leg of the pizza delivery guy. To this dog, she thinks she's helping and keeping the owner safe yet she's crossing the line. In the same way, anxiety comes in as a survival response on sensing a supposed threat in a bid to keep us alive. Most times, however, the supposed threat is not usually real.

In dealing with anxiety, a helpful manner is to act and behave in a way that will disarm it. In other words, let your response to the nervousness be that it is not needed. Bear in mind that your response to anxiety fuels it. The more you dread a snake, the more you feel terrified at the sight of one. However, if you see a snake and just act normal, your nervousness will disappear. That is the idea of this point, acting in a way that does not denote real emergency will make anxiety fade. For instance, should there be an emergency; there is not a chance that you will:

- Smile
- Salivate
- Talk as you would normally
- Take in a deep breath
- Have a relaxed posture

The idea is that adopting these behaviors, even if it is just one of them during the time of anxiousness or nervousness will alter the feedback mechanism. In other words, the feedback to our fear response system will change. Thus, we are telling our sympathetic nervous system: hey there, if there were a real threat, I wouldn't be this relaxed, talking normally, eating, chewing, taking a deep breath, etc.

No matter how hard the anxiety grips you, a simple action like chewing (you do not need anything in your mouth) will go a long way to help. Since this is something you will not do should there be a real threat?

Should there be a serious life-threatening situation that could cause panic (a terrorist attack or tsunami for instance) there is no chance you will take a deep breath, salivate or assume a relaxed posture. This is a tactic that can produce instant calm when faced with threatening situations. The idea is altering the feedback loop in a bid to switch off anxiety. This can bring a terrific boost in confidence and help ease anxiety.

iii. Examine the Assumption and Readjust the Conclusion

Most times, anxiety about something is due to a fear of the consequence. In dealing with anxiety, what is the consequence?

- If I am afraid of making a thesis defense presentation, "what exactly

am I afraid of"
- I might assume, I fear the people I will meet
- And the consequence of that: they might judge me wrongly
- And the consequence of that: I might be upset
- And the consequence of that: I will feel like a failure

This can go on and on. But how do we deal with this

Examining the worst that can go wrong will go a long way in helping. In other words, for the candidate above, even if people judge him wrongly, with time, many people will move on with their life and forget about the thesis presentation.

On another hand, nothing that nothing is permanent and that some memory fades too quickly from people can make all the difference. In other words, the kind of expectation you assume for something might be wrong and exaggerated. However, taking the time to examine other positive ways in which the circumstance can go will go a long way in working against anxiety response.

Chapter Summary

We have examined helpful and practical steps you can take to calm anxiety instantly. As a recap, bear the following in mind:

i. Reframing thoughts can be very useful
ii. Feelings are not constant but subjected to change. Hence, any unpleasant feelings will surely pass.
iii. Altering behavioral feedback can go a long way in disrupting the anxiety feedback mechanism. With this, if we act normal and anxiety has nothing to feed on, it will stand down.

We can also teach people surviving mechanism should what they dread to happen. They can also realize that it is not the end of the world.

CHAPTER 9: LIFESTYLE CHANGES TO TAKE BACK CONTROL

When anxiety disorder attacks, it could be like the entire world is crashing down on you. It is a horrible emotion that leaves you helpless in the face of a false danger. Anxiety arises as a result of uncontrolled thoughts which might be difficult to break free. The good news, however, is that you can make positive lifestyle changes to fight anxiety, rather than having to deal with it the rest of your life.

Bear in mind that lifestyle choices have a lot to play in managing anxiety. There are many habits that we develop over time that ends up fueling our anxiety. Many people for instance, in a bid to cope with stress resort to smoking. This, unknown to them, helps anxiety thrive. Binge eating, feeding on sugar and fast food when stressed also does not help anxiety in any way. From choosing to eat healthy to understanding the importance of deep breathing, there are many small changes you can engage to fight anxiety. The good news is that these are lifestyle changes that will bring an overall improvement in health. Be sure to commit to them and watch the amazing transformation in your life.

1. Get Adequate sleep

By adequate sleep, I mean at least seven hours of deep and restful sleep. One of the offspring of anxiety is insomnia. It is not surprising as your thought is considering every possible way things could go. This is why anxiety and sleeplessness go hand in hand. However, getting a good night's sleep can help keep anxiety at bay.

To get a good night's sleep, you can take creative steps to improve your sleep. Take a cue from the steps highlighted below:

- Have a cold shower before going to bed.
- Drink a glass of warm milk before bed
- Make your bedroom free from noise and all forms of distractions before sleeping
- Have a sleep schedule and keep to it
- Make sure your room is well ventilated
- The temperature of your room should not be extreme
- Do not sleep with blue light. Use dim light if you can't sleep without light.
- Avoid all screens (mobile phone and TV set) at least 30 minutes before going to bed
- Once it is noon, stop the use of caffeine. It affects the quality of sleep.
- Do not exercise in the evening; stop anything that can significantly stress you. If you must exercise, have yoga.

- Do not eat late into the night. If you must eat, take light foods that are easy to digest. We recommend honey or MCT oil.
- Have your mobile device in silent or Do Not Disturb Mode
- Take a magnesium supplement.

2. Avoiding Working at Home

One of the major sources of stress and anxiety for a lot of people is their job. The pressure from the job takes its toll on their mental health, triggering stress and anxiety. With this in mind, be sure to have a work-life balance. Desist from checking emails and taking work-related messages once you are home. Give yourself time to relax and catch up with your partner or kid.

Make sure you do not avoid going on vacation. It is a good avenue to let go of work stress and recharge.

3. Pay Attention to Your Diet

Unknown to many, what you put inside your body also triggers anxiety. Some foods constantly keep the body in a toxic state. If you are fond of smoking and drowning your sorrow in alcohol, you are not helping your body. Even though alcohol might make you forget your sorrow for a little while, it stimulates anxiety in the long run.

In the body, one of the most active body parts is the brain. It needs a steady flow of nutrients to keep up with its function. When you feed poorly, the brain will not have the needed nutrients to function properly. As a result, your neurotransmitter will suffer, setting the stage for anxiety.

- Be sure to concentrate on a healthy diet filled with whole foods. Staying constantly hydrated will help you as well. Your meals should be low in Tran's fats with enough calcium. Be sure to reduce caffeine, processed foods, refined sugar, and red meat. Rather, we recommend fruits, nuts, legumes, and seeds.

- Make sure you reduce sweetened beverages from your meals. Your tea should not be full of sugar. Cut off soda, fruit punch as they fuel anxiety and depression
- Try and go Decaf: excessive use of caffeine is also one of the leading causes of anxiety. As a result, try decaffeinated coffee. If you are already addicted to coffee, try and reduce it gradually

4. Limit Your Use of Social Media

One of the leading causes of anxiety is the overconsumption of social media. If you are not careful, what social media presents to you can stress you, fueling your anxiety. For instance, there are opinions of people on various issues like religion, politics, personal issues, and current affairs. If you are not careful, seeing the family vacation of a friend can paint the wrong picture and give a false impression. It could make you think others have things going so well for them while you are struggling. This could lead to fear of missing out, fueling anxiety. This calls for being careful in what you allow to sink in while on social media.

5. Take Steps to Reduce Stress

Stress and anxiety go hand in hand. In other words, excessive stress comes from depression and anxiety. With this in mind, one of the best things you can do for yourself is to take time to manage and get rid of stress. Be sure to learn healthy coping mechanisms to deal with stress. Even though alcohol might make you forget your worries and troubles for a while, it does not help in the long run. We discuss the following tips to beat stress

- Take note of the source of stress in your life and take healthy stress to address them. Stressors could be responsibilities, unfulfilling relationships, etc. When you know this, you can take a positive step to address them.

- Music has a huge capacity to relax the body. No matter how stressed you are, soothing music can help calm your nerves. Form a habit of listening to music as it has a soothing effect on mental health.
- When you are stressed, you take a short, shallow breath. Try and take long breaths however because it helps increase air circulation forcing the body into a state of relaxation.

6. Get in Touch with Nature

You are not helping yourself if you spend eight hours at work with a full air conditioning system. You close at work also, walk to your car and drive home, still with the car Ac blowing. You do not take time to enjoy natural breeze and vitamin D from the sun. It is not surprising that anxiety thrives in this condition.

Be sure to take a walk in the park. Go for sightseeing, go to the zoo and spend time appreciating the gift of nature. Even if you live in the city, there should be parks you can visit. Better still, have a garden, get your hands dirty tilling the ground. Not only will this keep you busy leaving no space for anxiety at all, but it will also help you get your hands dirty. This is also a way to get access to some minerals.

7. Make Sure Your Home is Clutter-Free

One of the major sources of stress and anxiety is a clutter. We are all guilty of this as there are things in our life and home we hold on to that are not that useful. There are clothes we have not worn in years that are still in our wardrobe. We hold on to items for no tangible reason. Yet, things like this only end up fueling anxiety.

Remember the last time you were looking for something, only to find it between piles of rubble on your home. This is something you will not have to look for had your home been free of clutters. This is more than maintaining a clean home. It is about getting rid of unnecessary items from your home. Sentimental items, historical items, etc., that you do not need does not help you in any way.

Make sure you go from room to room and get rid of everything you haven't used in a while. Donate to charity, sell them or dispose of them. You will feel good and live in good health, reducing the impact of anxiety.

8. Meditate

We get anxious over things we have no control on. We worry, ruminate, access and obsess over matters which take its toll on our mental health. We consider various scenarios in which things can go wrong. Anxiety makes us get lost in various unhelpful thoughts.

When you meditate, however, you bring back your thought to the moment. Rather than getting all worked up on something you have no control over, meditation helps you focus on something you can control- your breath.

We recommend starting your day off with some minutes of meditation with your breathing as the focal point. It is not something tedious, breath in and out consciously for five times, focusing on your breath. That is meditation at its simplest form.

9. Get Social Support

Anxiety thrives with anxiety and loneliness. As a result of this, you need to create a healthy support system around you to beat anxiety. Besides, your circle of friends and loved ones should not be critical people that will get you worked up always.

It is also tempting to want to stay away from people when anxious. Friends are helpful as they can help us make a realistic assessment of the threat and offer comfort. Besides family and friends, a support group can help you realize that you are not alone. You also get to learn from the experience of others as well as their coping mechanism. Besides joining a support group, you can keep in touch with families and friends. Getting a pet, dog or cat, for instance, will also go a long way to help.

10. Practice Self Care

You are an individual that matters. You are the most important person in your universe. You deserve the best, irrespective of what the voices in your head are saying. Be sure not to neglect yourself. Get a good haircut, invest in a massage, get a pedicure and a manicure, etc. Go to the sauna with a friend. Do not ditch a night out with the girls. Get yourself something you like, give yourself a treat. This can go a long way in helping you rise above anxiety.

11. Get a Strong sense of purpose

In other words, have something you live for. You should not just live life as it comes. With a strong sense of purpose, you are better equipped to handle all that life throws at you without sinking into anxiety and depression. Besides, a strong sense of purpose is like a shield against the ups and downs of life.

With a strong sense of purpose, you will be satisfied with life even in difficult days. This can prevent you from sinking into anxiety.

12. Make Exercise a Daily Habit

One of the most important steps you can take to fight anxiety and take back control is exercise. Exercise can improve mood, reduce the release of stress hormones and make you feel good overall. You do not have to work out like a maniac or register at the local gym. A simple exercise plan like yoga, walking, tai chi can improve your mood significantly, leaving no place for anxiety.

Exercise is helpful as it boosts the secretion of endorphins and serotonin. These are brain chemicals that fight depression and anxiety. A simple 30-

minute walk per day will go a long way in lifting your mood. Besides helping with anxiety, exercise is a good way to get your life in order, fight disease and be in good health.

13. Attempt Positive Statements

We get anxious since we are trying to examine various ways in which things can go wrong. However, when you counter this with positive thoughts and statements, it can help lift your mood and fight anxiety. Not only will this help overcome negative thought, but you also get to put things into perspective and lift your spirit.

Chapter Summary

Your day to day choices, without a doubt, has a long way to go in fueling anxiety. However, you can choose to make choices that will keep anxiety at bay. From the food you eat to how you take care of yourself to the company you keep; you can take helpful steps to keep anxiety at bay.

CHAPTER 10: PANIC ATTACKS

If you have witnessed or had a panic attack before, you will know how terrible, exhausting and overwhelming it is. It is in the class of anxiety disorder that leaves victims feeling helpless amid strong surging emotions.

A panic attack is a sudden burst of great fear, dread, and discomfort which springs up within a few minutes. It is characterized by a variety of physical and psychological symptoms. Symptoms of panic attacks are:

- Intense heart rate or palpitation
- Sweating,
- Strong fidgeting and trembling
- Shortness of breath,
- Hot flashes,
- Lightheadedness
- Nausea,

- Feeling of choking
- Chest pain, headache, and or
- Abdominal pain,
- Numbness
- Fear of dying
- Fear of going insane
- Feeling dizzy
- Tingling, etc.

When someone is a victim of constant, unexpected panic attacks, it is termed as panic disorder. Many times, the attack is sudden or unexpected. Most times as well, panic attacks occur in the presence of a trigger like generalized anxiety disorder or phobia.

Causes of Panic Disorder

Research has yet to pinpoint a specific cause for panic disorder. However, from studies, a panic attack occurs as a result of some factors like environmental stresses and biology. People that usually experience negative emotions, people with anxiety disorder have a high risk of developing panic disorder. Some of these factors are:

1. ***Family History:*** in other words, the panic disorder could be hereditary. The same way eye color, diseases, etc., are passed from parents to offspring, the panic disorder occurs in a family line. Although, the exact gene and gene product responsible for panic attack and panic disorders are not known. However, if mental health issues like depression, bipolar disorder, anxiety disorder, etc., run in your family, there is a high risk of developing panic disorder.

2. ***Biological Malfunction:*** Some malfunction and abnormalities in the brain, neurotransmitters and nervous system can also be

responsible for panic disorders.

3. ***Major life Stress***: Major, traumatic life events and stress can also cause the panic disorder. The death of a loved one, witnessing a horrible event like an earthquake, terrorist attack, etc. Childhood experience of physical or sexual abuse can also trigger the panic disorder.
4. ***Substance Abuse***: excessive reliance on drugs and alcohol can also cause panic attacks.

Understanding Panic Attacks

A panic attack comes with many distressing and overwhelming symptoms as listed above. The experience is usually terrifying that the victim believes they are dying. At times, people also confuse it for heart attack. The panic attack also makes the victim feel like they are no longer in control of themselves and their body. It creates an embarrassing scene with a feeling of impending doom.

Most times, the attack is unexpected and characterized by at least four of the symptoms highlighted above. Many times, as well, panic attacks occur in the presence of a phobia. In other words, someone that has experienced a terrorist hostage situation at the mall could experience a panic attack on their next visit to the mall.

The duration of the panic attack differs from people. Generally, however, a panic attack reaches its peak within 10 minutes. They usually last for an average of 30 minutes but the symptoms will generally subside in 10 minutes.

Finding Instant Calm for Panic Attack

Kindly note that there are recommended treatments for panic disorders. More of this will be discussed in the coming sections. However, if you are looking for instant calm for a panic attack, this section will discuss the important techniques that can be of great help.

1. Employ Deep breathing

One of the signs of intense stress is shortness of breath. This is because of the unrest of the body which increases fear. However, when you breathe deeply, it can go a long way to reduce the symptoms of panic attacks. One of the keys to getting panic attacks in check is by controlling your breathing. If you can control it, you can keep a panic attack in check.

Focus on sucking in air through your mouth and nose. Let the air fill your entire stomach and body and allow it to escape gradually. If possible, practice some simple breathing meditation by making a count of four after sucking in air and breathing out again.

2. Know that it is Only a Panic Attack

The symptoms of a panic attack can be so strong, overwhelming and intense that some people confuse it for something else. They assume they are dying or they are having a heart attack. However, the key here is reminding yourself that it is an ordinary panic attack and that is all. Your life is not being snuffed out by some unseen forces.

In other words, no matter how intense the feeling, it will surely pass. If you get rid of the fear that you are dying or the world is ending, the effect of the symptoms will die down. With this, you can focus on practical steps to combat the attack.

3. Close Your eyes

Many times when people have panic attacks, they are usually facing to face triggers (phobia for instance) that overwhelms them. If there are many stimuli in your environment as well, it can fuel the attack.

To reduce the impact of the attack, be sure to have your eyes closed. This way, you are blocking out any external source of stimuli that might make the attack intense. With this, you can concentrate solely on controlling your breathing.

4. Practice Mindfulness

Mindfulness brings you back to the moment. Rather than getting carried away in the fear of what might happen or what is going to happen, mindfulness grounds you in the reality of your present environment. Many people while having a panic attack do feel they are under the influence of some unseen forces. However, you can correct this with mindfulness.

You can practice simple mindfulness like stroking your thumb and noting how it makes you feel. It could also be as simple as noticing how your denim feels on your thigh. These are simple sensations that keep you in touch with the present reality, giving you a focus, rather than getting carried away by your sensations.

5. Find a Focal Point

In other words, find an object to focus on when you feel the panic rising within you. Like a laser, direct your focus on that specific thing or object to distract you from the sensation rising from within you. Be meticulous about the object and note every little detail about it.

For instance, assuming you are in a vehicle, you could take notice of the driver. Watch how he is focused on the road. Notice how he maneuvers the steering and engages the gears at the interval. Notice how he's not interested in anything but the road. With all your energy directed at this person, your panic attack will evaporate gradually.

6. Employ Muscle Relaxation Technique

During panic attacks, the body responds as if an apparent danger is imminent. With a muscle relaxation technique, however, you can address and stop panic attacks by checking the natural response your body is giving out.

All it involves is consciously relaxing one muscle at a time and moving to the other parts of your body. For muscle relaxation tips to be effective, you must have been practicing them beforehand.

7. Employ Visualization

In other words, with your mind, picture the most relaxing place you can think of. It could be somewhere in the Bahamas, a beach in Hawaii or the Caribbean. It could be somewhere you have been before or where you always longed to be. We recommend a calm, gentle and relaxing atmosphere, and not the ever-busy streets of urban life.

Picture yourself there and focus on the details. Imagine surfing on the waters of Hawaii and enjoying a local dish of Shrimp. Imagine relaxing on the beach while the ocean breeze caresses your body. The beauty is in the details.

8. Have a Mild Exercise

When you exercise, it releases endorphins which can keep the blood pumping just right. This goes a long way to improve mood and keep anxiety and panic attack in check. When under intense stress from a panic attack, we recommend mild exercise like walking or swimming if possible.

If you are, however, struggling with your breath, catching your breath should be the priority and not exercise.

9. Have an Internal Mantra

Having a mantra is another way to meditate. It gives you something to focus on, rather than being carried away by your symptoms. A mantra can relax and calm your muscles, giving you something to hold on to with the attack.

It can be a phrase as simple as "I am in control," or "This too shall pass." Repeat this mantra in your head and watch out for the symptoms of the attack to die down.

10. Have Lavender Handy

If you are prone to a panic attack, having some lavender oil handy will be of great help. Lavender essential oil can help calm your nerves during the time of panic attacks. Simply breathing in the scent during the time of the attack will go a long way in soothing you.

Be aware that the tips recommended here are just options you can use to calm yourself down in the face of a panic attack. They are not long term treatment options. The next section will shed light on a treatment option for panic disorder.

Cognitive Behavioral Therapy for Panic Disorders

Cognitive Behavioral Therapy revolves around the idea that it is our thoughts that influence our feelings and behaviors. Rather than something or someone external like people, events or situations controlling us, it is internal (our thoughts). CBT Therapy teaches us that if we can adjust how we think, our feelings also can change in response which can happen even if external circumstances do not change.

Cognitive Behavioral Therapy focuses on examining the behavior and thought patterns that trigger and sustain the panic attack. It employs a variety of cognitive and behavioral techniques to bring about changes in victims. It has been proven to be pretty effective hence it gives a quick result and is goal-oriented.

What Is Cognitive Behavioral Therapy?

Also known as CBT, it is a form of psychotherapy that helps provide relief to mental health. Cognitive Behavioral Therapy teaches that even though someone might not be able to change their life circumstances, they can change and adjust their reaction to the ups and downs of life.

Cognitive Behavioral Therapy also aims to adjust someone's unhealthy thinking pattern to curb unhealthy behaviors. There are many mental health conditions that CBT can handle such as phobia, addiction, post-traumatic stress disorder (PTSD), etc.

Understanding Cognitive Behavioral Therapy Treatment for Panic Attacks

One of the central goals of CBT is to help people curb negative thinking habits. With this, they are equipped to make the right decisions. People that suffer from panic disorders are pretty prone to negative thinking. They are also characterized by self-defeating thoughts which fuel anxiety and make the attack pronounced. Negative thinking and intense dread go hand in hand with a panic attack.

Cognitive Behavioral Therapy can help people with panic disorder develop healthy coping mechanisms to manage their symptoms. While the victim, most of the time, has no control over the time the panic attack strikes, he can take helpful steps to control and cope with the symptoms. CBT offers help for panic disorder victims via a two-part process which will be examined.

Recognize and Replace Negative Thoughts

One of the first assignments of the CBT therapist is to help victims recognize their negative thinking patterns. This usually involves asking the client to ruminate on how he perceives himself and the world around during the period of the attack. Focusing on this can make the person understand his thinking pattern and the influence it has on his behaviors.

CBT often involves various activities and exercises to help the client notice their faulty thought pattern and replace it with a healthy thinking pattern. There will be an additional task in the form of homework which will help clients identify and get rid of unhelpful thoughts.

Writing exercise is one of the activities to get rid of unhelpful thinking patterns. The client can use this to keep tabs on their thought and catch unhelpful thoughts. Some forms of CBT writing exercise are journaling, having a panic diary, and keeping a gratitude journal, etc.

Skill Building and Behavioral Changes

After recognizing the pattern of unhealthy thought, the next step is to focus on healthy coping skills to address and change maladaptive behaviors. This is where the client learns a helpful skill to cope with stress, reduce anxiety and survive panic attacks. The client, with the help of the CBT therapist, can learn and rehearse the skills.

One of the CBT skills learned is desensitization which helps the client overcome avoidance behaviors. The aim is to help clients come face to face with their fear without triggering the symptoms of a panic attack. This happens via systematic desensitization. In other words, the therapist introduces the clients gradually to their specific panic triggers while helping them come up with helpful ways to cope with the symptoms.

The client also learns relaxation techniques which is essential for remaining calm through all the panic-provoking periods. With these skills, victims learn to reduce tension, manage fear, reduce their heart rate and develop adequate problem-solving skills. Some relaxation techniques are progressive muscle relaxation, deep breathing exercises, mindfulness, and yoga.

Chapter Summary

A panic attack is real and dangerous. However, you can take helpful steps to get your symptoms in check during the episode of the attack. Better still, CBT provides a helpful approach to find a permanent solution to panic disorder.

Your recovery will not come in a day but you can work with your CBT therapist to reduce the symptoms and get the attack in check when it strikes.

CHAPTER 11: PHOBIAS

Almost everyone is guilty of irrational fear – of snake, insect, germs, needles, spider, the elevator, etc. This fear, for many people, is minor which is normal. You might not need treatment if you dread snakes for instance. However, there are times, the fear gets so severe that it interferes with your normal life, triggering uncontrollable anxiety to the point where it embarrasses you. This is called a phobia.

A phobia is a great fear of something an object, a place, or someone (clown.) While in reality, the source of dread is of no imminent threat to the safety of the person. Even though most phobias develop in childhood, many adults also experience phobias.

One thing common with many people with a phobia is the realization that their fear is baseless, but they are helpless. Mere thinking about their object of dread could make them anxious. Real exposure to feared objects triggers great terror and sometimes panic attacks. The experience is so overwhelming that people go to great lengths to avoid their source of fear. Someone with a fear of flying, for instance, might turn down a lucrative job offer that involves traveling around to meet clients. In other words, phobia makes victims inconvenience themselves and go to great lengths to avoid it.

Comparing Normal fears and Phobias

It is normal and sometimes helpful to be fearful in the presence of a dangerous situation. This can be traced back to the period of our forefathers. Their lives in the primitive period were characterized by chasing animals and running away from predators. As a result, they need to constantly activate their fight-or-flight" response, as it could mean the difference between life and death. The body interprets any dangerous thing as a potential source of threat hence in a bid to keep us alive, it activates the fear or flight response. This manifest as severe anxiety in man

However, we are no more running away from lions. Yet, every source of threat is met with the same reaction as that of our forefathers. In the presence of a real source of the threat, fear serves as a protective mechanism meant to keep us alive. There are times when the body, however, gives an exaggerated estimation of the threat level. For instance, it is normal to be fearful when a flight is turbulent. To however avoid going to a party because you have to fly is a phobia.

Signs and Symptoms of Phobia

From mild anxiety to a full-blown panic attack, the symptoms of phobia vary. In general, the closer someone is to their source of dread, the more intense the fear. Also, if escape is difficult, the feeling of terror will be great. Physical symptoms of anxiety are:

- Problem with breathing

- Racing heart
- Sweating
- Chest tightness and pain
- Intense trembling
- Feeling dizzy

On the other hand, emotional symptoms of phobia are:

- Experiencing a panic attack
- Feeling detached or away from yourself
- Feeling like life is passing out of you
- The consciousness of over-reacting but being helpless to control

Seeking help for Phobia

Almost everyone has one or two objects that they dread. However, in many cases, phobias do not always cause a significant disruption in day to day living. For instance, if you have a fear of clown, you might not have to worry about running into a clown. In the same way, if you have a phobia for a cluster of circles and small holes, it might not be a problem as long as the likelihood of running into them is slim. However, a phobia becomes an issue when it interferes with day to day living. Fear of flying will be a big deal for a salesman who has to travel many kilometers to close deals.

The idea is that as long as your day to day living is not affected, you might not be concerned. You should seek help if the fear of the object keeps you from living life and doing what is expected of you. In short, you need treatment for your phobia if:

- It triggers excessive trembling, fear and anxiety
- It causes a panic attack
- You know your reaction is exaggerated and not proportionate to the feared object

- You keep away from people, places, and situations because of the fear.
- The avoidance behavior affects your day to day routine
- The phobia has been with you for at least five months.

How to treat a Phobia

If you have established that you need help with your phobia, there are self-help techniques and other therapies that can help. When you consider the intensity of your phobia, and how much support you need, you can decide the type of treatment you need.

You can always attempt self-help if you feel up to the task. If you can help yourself with the phobia, you will be more in control. For a phobia that makes you numb and triggers a panic attack, we recommend getting professional help.

Therapy for addressing phobia gives fast results and is very effective. Many clients report seeing a result from the forth section. The best part is that you might not need to talk to a therapist. Having a loved one help you through the crisis period or when you feel powerless can go a long way in helping you overcome this.

Self Help Tips for Phobia

Step 1: Face Your Fears Gradually

By instinct, we tend to avoid what we fear. This is because we consider avoidance as an escape from the object of dread. Yet, while this provides temporary comfort, it prevents you from coming to terms with the fact that the feeling of dread is exaggerated. To conquer your fear, however, the major key is facing it. This helps you cope with it, giving you the chance to develop tactics to survive.

With gradual, controlled and repeated exposure however, you can overcome your fear. The exposure process teaches you to rise above the anxiety until you no longer feel helpless. With continuous exposure, you get to realize that your world will not come crashing down and there is no worst that will happen. Each exposure increases your confidence level and puts you more in control.

We recommend starting small. In other words, start with something you can handle. From there, increase the intensity and build your confidence and coping skills with each exposure.

Have a List: In other words, make a list of situations surrounding your phobia. For instance, if you are afraid of visiting a dentist, your list might include things like:

- Seeing the dentist office
- Knocking on the dentist's door
- Talking to the dentists
- Seeing the dentist's pieces of equipment
- Listening to the dental procedures
- Lying on the dentist's chair etc.

Have a Hierarchy of fear: Have an arrangement of things on your list from the least scary to the terrifying ones. The first item on your list should give you chills but not make you intimidated enough to avoid it. Be sure to always have your end goal in mind while having your hierarchy of fear. For instance, a goal could be to walk up to a stranger and have a smooth conversation without making a fool of yourself. Your steps on your hierarchy should contribute to your overall goal.

Consider Each Item on Your List: The key is starting with the first step and getting used to it. The longer you stay there, the more comfortable you feel and the lesser the effect of the dreaded object/place on you. Once a particular step feels comfortable, you can proceed to the next one. Should there be any overwhelming step along the way; break it down into smaller steps. In time, you stop giving exaggerated reactions to the source of the dread.

Practice: Practice helps you have swift progress. Be sure not to rush yourself, however. Moving at a comfortable pace is very vital. Feeling overwhelmed might affect your progress hence take it easy. Feeling of discomfort and anxiety will surely rise when facing your fear. The more you, however, stand face to face with your fear, the more you discover that your feelings are temporal and the panic will evaporate.

Dealing with Pteromerhanophobia (Fear of Flying): Using the Hierarchy of Fear

   i. Step 1: Look at pictures of airplanes
   ii. Step 2: Look at pictures of airports
   iii. Step 3: Watch lots of videos of people in aircraft and airplane flying
   iv. Step 4: Look at an aircraft in the sky
   v. Step 5: Visit the airport and watch airplanes on the tarmac
   vi. Step 6: If possible, enter an aircraft that is not going to take off
   vii. Step 7: Play a flight simulator game
   viii. Step 8: Pay for a short distance flight

If you feel extremely overwhelmed, do not beat yourself up. That is a tip for you to back off immediately and proceed to the next step that discusses how to relax in the presence of distressing triggers.

Step 2: Learn the Coping technique

The main reason we suggested that you back off in the example above is based on the assumption that you have not learned coping mechanisms. Without a doubt, there will be a surge in uncomfortable emotions and physical sensations in the presence of a phobia trigger. Victims could experience a racing heart, intense trembling, and dizziness. These are part of what makes the phobia overwhelming. The key, however, is in learning ways to calm your nerves such that you remain unshaken while facing your fears. Simple tips to make this possible are:

Try and Breathe Deeply. Anxiety is characterized by the inability to take deep breaths. Due to the effect of the panic on the body, the body is tensed, unable to breathe in deeply. This, also known as hyperventilating helps fuel anxiety. When you, however, take deep breaths from the abdomen, it disturbs the anxiety feedback mechanism thereby reversing the sensations and reduces tension. The following steps help you with a quick deep breathing exercise. You can attempt this when you are less stress to get the hang of it.

i. Stand or sit comfortably with a straight back.
ii. Take a deep and slow breath through your nose, making a count to four.
iii. Hold the breath for a count of seven
iv. Exhale through your mouth and make a count of seven. Force out as much air as you can while constricting your abdominal muscle.
v. Inhale again repeating this cycle till you are relaxed and grounded.

For five minutes, practice this deep breathing exercise. It will come in handy when you are face to face with your phobia.

Employ your Senses: One of the best ways to beat anxiety and let it evaporate is by engaging any of the five senses – the sense of touch, smell, sight, taste, sound, and even movement. However, this involves practice to know the one that works for you.

i. Movement: Stretch, go for a walk, jump, leave where you are, etc.
ii. Sight: Look at something, anything that calms your nerves.
iii. Sound: Listen to your favorite music or have some relaxing background tones playing
iv. Smell: spray your favorite perfume, breath in a scented candle, etc.

v. Taste: sip a coffee, have a mint or chew gum. It helps.

vi. Touch: massage your thumb or cuddle a little furry friend if you have one – a cat or puppy

Step 3: Challenge Negative Thoughts that come with the Phobia

One of the reasons phobia triggers intense panic is because we exaggerate the intensity of the situation. This amplifies the fear and cripples all our coping mechanisms, making us feel helpless. A careful examination of the thoughts responsible for phobia will reveal that they are unreal and negative. When you put these thoughts down in writing, you can examine the thought pattern and determine if they are helpful. Many at times, these sorts of thoughts fall into the following categories:

Fortune telling: there is going to be another terrorist attack at the mall. There will be a gunman shooting sporadically at the bank today. I will pass out once the airplane hits turbulence.

Overgeneralization: I once fumbled and lost my voice while trying to talk to a beautiful lady. I will never be able to talk to a girl I like again. The was power failure in the last elevator I was and we were trapped for hours. The next elevator I will enter will also face the same situation.

Catastrophizing: the ship captain said there is a Northwind approaching. This ship is going down. I saw a mosquito in my room. I am getting the flu soon.

On identifying the negative thought, the next step is to challenge and evaluate them with facts. Take a cue from the following:

Negative Thought Sample: I will pass out once the plane hits turbulence.

To combat this negative thought, ask yourself the following question:

- What is the evidence that contradicts this thought?
- There have been reports of many planes hitting turbulence and making it.

- The pilots are trained to maneuver the airplane to scale through turbulence
- There is parachute to convey people to the ground should things get out of hand.

Is this a thinking error?
- Yes, since there is no evidence to support the fact that once the plane hits turbulence, it is going down.

How will you comfort a friend with this fear?
- I would probably tell him pilots are trained at handling turbulence hence it is not a cause for alarm.

Chapter Summary

Without a doubt, a phobia is a false fear that can affect the way you live your life. However, the most important step in overcoming a phobia is facing it. Even though it will be overwhelming, it is the key to breaking free of the shackles of anxiety and panic that comes from a phobia. With the teachings of this chapter, you can break free from the unseen forces holding you captive.

CHAPTER 12: SOCIAL ANXIETY

It is normal and expected to have some level of nervousness when meeting someone for the first time, facing a crowd or interviewing for a job. Social anxiety, however, is way past temporary shyness. It is more about intense dread for social situation to the extent of avoiding it. This happens mostly in situations when you will be watched or judged by people.

Many people with social anxiety live under the dread that they will be judged, scrutinized which could lead to embarrassment. Victims assume that they might not measure up to standard which leads to anxiety. Many times, victims know that their fear is irrational, yet they are helpless about the anxiety. The good news is that you can take helpful steps to get the anxiety in check.

Signs and Symptoms of Social Anxiety

It should be noted that shyness and feeling of discomfort are different from social anxiety disorder. Depending on someone's personality traits and life experience, the level of comfort in social situation varies. An introvert, for instance is more reserved even in day to day interaction, compared to an extrovert.

Social anxiety on the other hand stands out. It is characterized by fear, anxiety, dread and outright avoidance of social situations which interferes with day to day living, school, relationship, etc. As a result, people with this disorder avoid simple day to day experience like making eye contact, dating, going to work or school, asking questions in public, going to the restroom, attending social gathering, eating in front of others, returning something to the store etc.

Behavioral and Emotional symptoms

- Concerned about humiliating yourself in public
- Dreadful feeling of talking to strangers
- Anxiety when you think about a social event,
- Stopping yourself from doing things before people because of fear of embarrassing yourself
- Staying away from situations where you have the spotlight on you
- Worrying that others will notice your anxiety

Physical Symptoms of anxiety include:

- Trembling
- Racing heart
- Nausea
- Sweating
- Lightheadedness
- Difficulty catching your breath

Causes of Social Anxiety

The cause of social anxiety disorder can be traced to a complex interaction of environmental and biological factors. Some causes are:

Inherited Factors: There is a big possibility that anxiety disorder runs in family line. It might be due to genetics or learned behavior.

Brain Structure: If you have a hyper active amygdala, there is a huge chance you will develop social anxiety. Amygdala is that part of the brain that controls fear response.

Environment: Someone whose voice failed them after an attempt to ask question in a public setting might detest asking question again especially if it led to embarrassment. In other words, social anxiety might arise as a result of embarrassing or unpleasant situation.

How to Overcome Social Anxiety

Many times, people are anxious socially because they think they will make a fool of themselves. In other words, it all starts from the thought. As a result, to get rid of social anxiety, we need to start from the root- the thoughts.

Technique 1: Challenge Negative Thoughts

Many people that suffer social anxiety have negative thoughts which tend to fuel their anxiety in social situation. For instance, they might have voices in their head that tells them:

- You will end up making a mess of the presentation
- Your voice will shake and people will laugh at you
- People will think you are fool
- You don't have anything interesting to say, people will think you are boring.

I bet you identify with this type of thoughts. We recommend the following steps:

Step 1: Identify the main negative thought behind your social anxiety. For someone worked up about a coming thesis defense, the main negative thought could be: "I will make a fool of myself, people will think I am a dullard."

Step 2: Examine and refute the negative thought. One effective way to accomplish this is asking question that examines the authenticity of the thoughts. For instance: "How sure am I that I will make a mess of the defense?" or "Does nervousness means that I am a dullard?"

With such a logical evaluation, it can open your eyes to realistic and positive ways of viewing the situation

Technique 2: Take the Focus off Yourself

We succumb to social situation because we are filled with thoughts, feelings and assumptions about ourselves. You are carried away with the thought that everyone is analyzing, evaluating and criticizing you. The problem with this kind of thinking is that it makes you focus on your anxiety, making you more nervous. As a result, your performance in social setting is affected since you are worried about people judging you.

With the above in mind, it makes sense to focus on others as it helps reduce anxiety. The more your attention centers on what is going on around you, the less you will be anxious of the situation.

- Focus on the person you are talking to, not on what they are thinking of you
- That someone notices you are anxious does not mean they will conclude you are a fool. There is a chance the person you are meeting is as nervous as you.
- Let go of the pressure to be perfect. Direct your attention on being genuine

Technique 3: Face Your fears

When you are anxious about something, there is a big chance you avoid that thing. What you do not know is that avoidance keeps the anxiety in check. To learn how to cope and handle social situation without your emotions going haywire, you need to change your approach. As a result of this, to really rise above social anxiety, you need to face the situation and circumstances that's making you anxious.

Besides preventing you from beating social anxiety, avoidance prevents you from achieving your goals and going for what you want. For instance, social anxiety might prevent you from a potential relationship when you cannot summon up the courage to walk up to, and talk to a lady you like at a party.

We understand that asking you to face your fear is an overwhelming step. This is where baby steps come in. Be sure to start with a situation you can handle and graduate to challenging situations. This way, you build your confidence level gradually.

For instance, if talking to a pretty lady scares the hell out of you, you can start by getting yourself more out there. Go to parties and club in the company of friends. In time, you could ask that your friend introduce you to their circle of friends and make conscious effort to stay in touch. Gradually, you will be able to introduce yourself to others and walk your way up.

Facing your greatest fear head on is a recipe for disaster. Try not to force things as it might not produce a good result.

Make sure you are patient with yourself. Social anxiety did not develop in a day, a week, or a month. Hence, it will take effort, dedication and persistent to overcome social anxiety.

Technique 4: Make the Effort to be Social

In other words, do not keep yourself from supportive social situations. We recommend the following steps that can help you interact with others positively

- Take a training class. It presents an opportunity to meet people and increase your circle of friends.

- Volunteer for a cause you love. It could be as simple as walking a dog, cleaning the adult's home etc. It doesn't have to be elaborate. As long as it gives you the chance to meet and talk to people in a relaxed environment, it will help.

- Develop your communication Skills. No matter the efforts you make to beat social anxiety, if your communication skill suck, your progress will slow down. Learn about emotional intelligence, connecting with others, developing empathy etc.

Technique 5: Chose a Lifestyle that Doesn't Support Anxiety

Unknown to many people, the way you treat your body influences your anxiety level significantly. In other words, how you treat yourself determines if you will build your confidence level, reduce anxiety level and beat the symptoms.

It should be noted that proper lifestyle support is only part of the equation in addressing social anxiety. With this in mind, we recommend the following lifestyle tips to beat social anxiety.

- Limit or Stay away from Caffeine: tea, soda, energy drinks and other source of caffeine are stimulants that fuels anxiety. It is a good idea to stay away from them or limit the intake

- Get Active: Physical activities increase the endorphin level. This reduces stress hormones which could fuel your anxiety. As little as

30 minutes of physical activities per day can help. It can be as simple as walking, brisk walking jogging and yoga.
- Stay Away from Smoking: Nicotine will not suppress your anxiety; rather it fuels it because it is a heavy stimulant. Take positive steps to stay away from smoking.
- Get Deep, and Quality Sleep: We are talking about getting deep and restful sleep. Because not getting enough sleep can fuel anxiety making you mess up in social situations.

Chapter Summary

Rather than allowing social anxiety to rob you of living life, you can take helpful steps to keep it in check. This chapter has discussed effective ways to beat social anxiety and be free.

CHAPTER 13: DEPRESSION LINK

Gradually, you are losing interest in everything. Even things that you once loved now irritate you. You just cannot find the pleasure in doing things you loved anymore.

The signs and symptoms of depression in people are pretty common. But feeling down after some major life crisis is perfect, normal and expected. For instance, one is bound to feel sad after losing a job or a baby. The problem comes when the person cannot snap out of this low state days or week after the event.

There are many things that cause depression in man. It could be a combination of biological and environmental factors. Genetics also contribute as well. Also, serotonin, a brain chemical plays a vital role in the onset of depression.

What is Depression?

Depression is one of the most common forms of mental health issues. Millions of people suffer depression which is characterized by the persistence of at least five of the nine symptoms for over two weeks. It is characterized by a great sadness and lack of interest in things that you love.

It should be noted that not all loss of interest and sadness can be classified as depression. As humans journey through life, there are experiences that will surely trigger unstable emotions. Depression is unique in that it lingers on for weeks, and months. It affects people of various ages and class.

Symptoms of Depression

There are many signs that characterize depression. Sadness is just a part of the equation and some people might not even feel sad when depressed. Depression influences both feelings and behavior of the victim. As a result, we will examine the signs of depression under psychological, behavioral and psychotic subheadings.

Psychological Symptoms of Depression

- Excessive shame
- Feeling of worthlessness
- Feeling of hopelessness
- Problem with concentration
- Loss of passion
- Unexplainable anxiety

Behavioral Symptoms of Depression

- Decreased energy level
- Emotional episodes like crying

- Loss of appetite
- Restlessness and irritability
- Social withdrawal
- Suicidal thoughts

Psychotic Symptoms

There are cases of depression in which the victim has a false sense of reality. This is characterized by incorrect thoughts that complement the mood. As a result, failures and other shortcomings in life will greatly affect the person.

Causes of Depression

Research is yet to uncover a specific cause for depression. However, genetic plays an important factor. Like other mental health issues, depression also runs in families.

Also, overwhelming and stressful life events also contribute to depression. General life conflicts and relationship stress also contributes to depression. Environmental and social stressors like childbirth, retirement, unemployment, loneliness, loss of someone dear or something also contribute to depression. These unpleasant life events could help trigger depression.

The character of a person also contributes to depression. Some people generally have a negative and faulty disposition to life events. These are people with depressive personality lifestyle which is characterized with a negative view of themselves and their situations. They hardly appreciate good things and are easily overwhelmed by the slightest onset of bad things.

Medications and illness also has a large role to play in the onset of depression. Thyroid hormones, hepatitis, birth control pills, anemia, diabetes, glandular fever, and influenza etc., could trigger symptoms of depression. Alcohol and abuse of some substance can also trigger symptoms of depression.

How to help Yourself out of Depression

Recovery from depression is a long process. While there are many treatment plan for depression, it takes time before any positive change comes up. In many patients, it might take up to months to record any positive progress on talking to a healthcare provider.

Antidepressant might bring about some positive changes, improving your mood after like three weeks. However, there are positive things you can do for yourself in the absence of medications and a medical practitioner.

Bear in mind that depression thrives because you allowed it. We understand that you lost your job but that doesn't mean you will not get another offer. Neither is this the end of your life. However, giving ears to negative thoughts that your life is over is a fuel for depression. If you, however, succumb to depression, there are positive steps you can take to feel better.

Take Baby Steps

One of the characteristics of depression is loss of interest in doing anything. Depression kills your desire in doing anything and your interest in being with people. However, not doing anything and staying away from people does not help. Rather get yourself out there, do something and even if you do not feel like. It is not about what you feel like doing but what you can do. It can be as simple as getting yourself up to do the dishes, taking care of the room or giving yourself a long and warm bath.

Due to depression, many people neglect themselves and the things expected of them. As a result, there might be piled up dishes, dirty cloths etc. Try and take up simple task like this, rather than huge and ambitious goals.

Whatever complex task you have to do, break it into smaller, achievable steps. This makes it less overwhelming and pretty easy to achieve. For instance, you might not have to jump right into washing your cloths. You could simply start by getting rid of clusters of dirty laundry flying around your bedroom. Pack it in preparation for laundry. The next day you might go to the mall and get the laundry detergent. The next day do the laundry while you press the cloths the following day. You might not have to do them consecutively as illustrated above. Move at a comfortable pace and not over exert yourself.

Try and Reactivate Relationships and Interest

With depression, people stay away from their social circles. However, making effort to get back in the game could be of great help. Again, we emphasize baby steps. You might lack the willpower to go to a party on your won. Going with a friend might help. Call a friend you have spoken to for long. Drop in on a friend with the excuse of returning something you borrowed.

Try and have a confidant that you can talk to daily. There should be someone you are sharing your challenges with. It does not have to be a therapist and it might not be physical contact. You could communicate via chat apps, emails etc.

We also recommend support group. In such a group, you meet people of like minds and learn their struggles over the years, as well as their coping mechanism. With a support group, you get to realize that you are not alone and depression should not mean an end of the world for you.

You should also try and think about what you once enjoyed and loved doing that you no longer do. Gradually, start doing these things even if the enjoyment seems absent. Think of this as rising above the depression. Hence, even if you have lost interest in these things, see them as a medicine that will produce result in time.

Make Exercise a Habit

Many people hardly have time to exercise even when they are not depressed, let alone with depression. Exercise, however, has a calming effect on the mood. When you engage in habits that take care of yourself during depression, it can help you rise above it.

When you are depressed, the energy level is considerably low which kills your interest or desire in doing anything. There are studies, however, that prove that exercise improves mood in depressed people. With this in mind, picking yourself up and getting out there can help rise above depression. It does not have to be something elaborate. It can be as simple as a walk to the park, running, brisk walking etc. To spice things up, go with a partner.

Exercise releases neuro chemicals in the brain called endorphins which improves mood. There are yoga poses that helps with depression. You can also try to meditate. Make this a habit and you will hardly have time to sink into depressive episodes. Be sure not to allow discouragement set in if you do not feel on top of the world after your exercise. Going for a walk will not immediately make you feel better or snap you out of depression. Making it a habit will, however, help in the long run.

Do Not beat Yourself Up

We understand some things did not go how you planned it which made you feel bad and critical. One thing you should bear in mind is you are not the cause of any of it, hence, beating yourself up will not solve anything. It only serves to fuel the symptoms of depression. The best thing is recognizing the fact that you need help.

With this in mind, after losing your baby, avoid the temptation to drown in self-pity. Rather, shower yourself with compassion. Nurture yourself with love and acceptance. Whatever happened to you that triggered depression must have happened to many people and they came out of the situation just fine.

Seek Clarity

Depression is characterized by negative thoughts about yourself, and life situations in general. For instances, you hear voices in your head saying you cannot get anything done right, you are a fool. However, clear thinking pattern is what you need to fight depression. This will help you override the negative thoughts and rise above depression.

This is not about some motivational talk. It is about realigning your thoughts towards reality. In other words, think about yourself in a fair way. Hence when the thought springs on you that you are failure for not being able to keep your job.

Try and test the idea with questions whether it is valid or not, for instance

- How true is this?
- What evidence do I have to support this?

Actions to Avoid

Depression makes people resort to unhealthy coping mechanism such as drinking, smoking, drug abuse all in a bid to get rid of the depression. However, drowning your sorrow in bottles of alcohol and other vices might only provide temporal relieve. In the long run, the depression will thrive. This paves the way for substance abuse which does not help in the long run.

While feeling depressed, avoid making any critical life changes. Leaving your job, going for a divorce, relocating etc., for instance is a bad idea except it is a critical situation. There are situations when depression is caused by bad job or stressful situation. This is an exception.

Making decision while depressed is a recipe for disaster because you are not in the right frame of mind. You need the symptoms to subside before you can think clearly.

CONCLUSION

Anxiety disorder comes in many forms with the capacity of robbing people countless things in life. As a result of this, you need to take conscious effort to fight anxiety. It holds you back, limiting you and acting as a barrier between you and your goals in life. It robs you of relationship and holds you from spreading your tentacles.

Many people moments before they die reflect on their life and regret the things they couldn't do. If you do not want to look back and regret missed opportunities and a restricted life, taking step to overcome your anxiety is an important key. Luckily, this manual is a workbook that has examined various forms of anxiety disorder with the aim of teaching you how to deal with it.

No matter your age, it is never too late to get whatever form of anxiety disorder troubling you in check. Be it phobia, panic attack, social anxiety, depression etc., we have shed light on them in this manual. Buried deep in you are valuable potentials. It will be a disaster to let this mental illness rob you of maximizing it.

It is high time you stopped allowing social anxiety prevent you from talking to the lady you have always eyed. You need to rise above your phobia of flying and launch out to international firms that will boost your career. Rise above the fear of speaking in social gathering and voice your idea to prevent that bright idea from dying. Many people are too occupied with their personal life than to capitalize on how you struggled to find your voice.

It is important to note that you have to be committed to getting your mental health in order. In other words, you will not experience overnight transformation. What I am saying is that you should not stop at reading all the techniques recommended in this book alone. Rather, take each chapter and work on it, or your specific anxiety disorder and work on the recommended steps and suggestions. If you are dedicated to this, in time, you will experience superb improvement. Getting rid of your specific anxiety disorder is a treatment on its own. Be sure to go at a pace you are comfortable with and be focused. Reflect on how interesting your life will be without that anxiety disorder and let that be your motivation.

As long as you can pay the price to get rid of whatever form of anxiety disorder that is affecting you, your life will be better off. Without a doubt, this will not come on a platter of gold but keep at it. You heart will race uncontrollably at times. Your voice might ail you. Every fiber of your being might scream at you to run away when faced with your fear. Keep it up and keep going. Even if you fail, you are getting their gradually.

You can beat anxiety disorder and get your life in order.

REFERENCES

https://www.verywellmind.com/how-is-aromatherapy-used-for-social-anxiety-disorder-3024210

https://www.webmd.com/balance/stress-management/aromatherapy-overview

https://www.acupuncturecouncilofireland.com/acupuncture-and-anxiety-a-good-match/

https://www.verywellmind.com/acupuncture-for-panic-disorder-2584273

https://anxietypanichealth.com/2017/11/22/10-reasons-acupuncture-can-ease-stress-anxiety/

https://www.unk.com/blog/3-instantly-calming-cbt-techniques-for-anxiety/

https://www.mentalhelp.net/anxiety/behavioral-therapies/

https://tinybuddha.com/blog/instantly-calm-stressful-situations/

https://medium.com/thrive-global/7-lifestyle-changes-that-helped-ease-my-anxiety-6141a6f85fd1

https://www.romper.com/p/21-lifestyle-changes-that-can-help-reduce-anxiety-56436

https://www.takingcharge.csh.umn.edu/what-lifestyle-changes-are-recommended-anxiety-and-depression

https://www.psycom.net/panic-attacks-panic-disorder-symptoms

https://www.healthline.com/health/how-to-stop-a-panic-attack

https://www.cogbtherapy.com/cbt-for-panic-attacks

https://www.verywellmind.com/cognitive-behavioral-therapy-2584290

https://www.helpguide.org/articles/anxiety/phobias-and-irrational-fears.htm

https://www.mayoclinic.org/diseases-conditions/social-anxiety-disorder/symptoms-causes/syc-20353561

https://www.helpguide.org/articles/anxiety/social-anxiety-disorder.htm

https://www.helpguide.org/articles/depression/depression-symptoms-and-warning-signs.htm

https://www.counselling-directory.org.uk/memberarticles/techniques-for-overcoming-anxiety-mindfulness-of-breatihing

https://www.everyday-mindfulness.org/3-quick-mindfulness-practices-to-overcome-worry-anxiety-and-panic/

https://us.humankinetics.com/blogs/excerpt/quality-of-movement-emotions

https://mind-globe.com/how-manage-anxiety-attacks/

https://www.artofmanliness.com/articles/eisenhower-decision-matrix/

https://www.mdlinx.com/internal-medicine/article/4090

https://www.ncbi.nlm.nih.gov/pubmed/29073398

https://www.mayoclinic.org/diseases-conditions/depression/in-depth/depression-and-exercise/art-20046495

https://www.psychologytoday.com/us/blog/emotional-fitness/200908/top-10-simple-tools-reduce-anxiety

CPSIA information can be obtained
at www.ICGtesting.com
Printed in the USA
LVHW051156101220
673819LV00032B/1833